Jung's Typology in Perspective

Jung's Typology in Perspective

REVISED EDITION

Angelo Spoto

FOREWORD BY
Robert A. Johnson

CHIRON PUBLICATIONS • WILMETTE, ILLINOIS

First edition published in 1989 by Sigo Press, Boston, Massachusetts.

Permissions

The Collected Works of C. G. Jung, trans. R. F. C. Hull. Bollingen Series XX, Vols. 1–20. Copyright © by Princeton University Press. Excerpts, cited passim, are reprinted by permission of Princeton University Press.

Myers-Briggs Type Indicator® and MBTI® are registered trademarks of Consulting Psychologists Press, Palo Alto, California.

"Homeric Hymn to Hermes" from *Homeric Hymns*, trans. Athannasakis. Copyright © 1976 by The Johns Hopkins University Press. Reprinted by permission of the publisher.

Kabir poems from *The Kabir Book* trans. by Robert Bly. Copyright © 1971, 1977 by Robert Bly. Reprinted by permission of Beacon Press and MacMillan Publisher's Limited.

"Moving Forward" and "A Walk" from *Selected Poems of Rainer Maria Rilke*, edited and translated by Robert Bly. Copyright © 1981 by Robert Bly. Reprinted by permission of HarperCollins Publishers, Inc.

Library of Congress Catalog Card Number: 94–48754

Printed in the United States of America.
Copyedited by Richard Weisenseel and Sandra Hazel.
Book design by Vivian Bradbury.
Cover design by D. J. Hyde.

Library of Congress Cataloging-in-Publication Data:

Spoto, Angelo.
    Jung's typology in perspective / Angelo Spoto. — Rev. ed.
      p.   cm.
    Includes bibliographical references and index.
    ISBN 0–933029–93–4 (pbk.) : $14.95
    1. Typology (Psychology). 2. Jung, C. G. (Carl Gustav),
1875–1961. 3. Typology (Psychology)—Testing. 4. Psychological
tests—United States—History. 5. Myers-Briggs Type Indicator.
    I. Title.
    BF698.3.S66   1995
    155.2'64—dc20   94–48754
                                             CIP

ISBN 0–933029–93–4

For my parents, Angelo and Lily

Steadfast love and faithfulness will meet,
righteousness and peace will kiss each other.

Psalm 85:10

Contents

Foreword

JUNG'S CLASSIC BOOK *Psychological Types* remains a remarkably insightful model of human personality in its most dramatic guise. Perhaps this is why it is a work that promises as many risks as it does rewards.

Of the many people who continue to be attracted to Jung's typology, the greatest warning goes to those who may naively use it to inhibit or dam up the creative flow of the human encounter. Typology should not be used in this way, in effect to short-circuit the overarching mystery that is the brunt of psychological reality. Rather, it should help open us up to one another and provide illuminations.

In a practical sense, in his clinical relationships with patients, Jung found that typology could help him account for, turn to, or offset, if necessary, the presence of his own strong personality. By knowing his own psychological truths, he felt he could better see and appreciate those of others. As it was the psychological truths of the individual patient toward which Jung worked, in partnership with the patient, this was no small accomplishment.

Angelo Spoto's interpretation of Jung's typology is both spirited and forthright in a sense which Jung could approve. This book is not an easy retelling of Jung's 1921 text. Instead, Mr. Spoto seeks to vivify Jung's original insights, eventually to throw the reader back on himself, to grapple with his own typological biases and energies. To this effort, Mr. Spoto brings imagination, wisdom, and compassion.

In the course of his book, we are treated to at least four perspectives on Jung's typology: first, a psycho-cultural perspective developed through an examination of the roots of Jung's typological theory and connecting to present-day interest in Jung's typology as represented through the Myers-

Briggs Type Indicator®. Second, we have a perspective gathered from an analysis of Jung's own typological research. In effect, this gives us a concise restatement of the working principles, dynamics, and terminology found in Jung's 1921 study. Third, we are treated to a perspective on Jung's own psychological type, worked out imaginatively in dialogue form between Jung and Jung's typological counterpart. Fourth, we have an excellent perspective on the place of typology within Jung's broader analytical work, clearly written for those interested in deepening their use of typology.

I was especially struck by Mr. Spoto's treatment of a key aspect of Jung's theory of types, namely the inferior function. I have understood the inferior function to be our "God connection," the psychological place where we can no longer bar the archetypal realities that are the true source of our being and becoming. Mr. Spoto provides the emphasis and recreates the drama for working with the inferior function in such psychologically compelling and challenging ways.

Finally, for those readers who have found Jung's own writings particularly dense and difficult, Mr. Spoto's book may make for a fruitful transition back to Jung's original work. Mr. Spoto's book reflects a constant awareness of Jung's works as a whole. His writing style is clear, vigorous, and balanced, yet he always allows enough room for the honest debate and discussion that will keep Jung's typology and psychology alive and well into the next century.

Robert A. Johnson

Robert A. Johnson is a Jungian analyst and author of the books *He, She, We,* and *Ecstasy*.

Preface to the Revised Edition

WHEN I COMPLETED THIS book in 1988, I wanted to introduce Jung's larger psychological model to the average reader in a way that I believed would be imminently practical, but without compromising the breadth and depth found in Jung's *Collected Works*. I found then and now that many people interested in the same issues Jung had been working with during his life took Jung's own impressive output to be quite unapproachable. Typical criticisms applied: he was too dense, too mystical, too intellectual, too demanding, too complex, too egotistical, too far-out, too impractical, too mythological, and so forth. The question I became interested in was, "How do I make Jung's work more accessible and practical and less intimidating for people who share Jung's interests?" My answer was to get in and out of the *Collected Works* by way of his typology.

I quickly found that a large number of people already were interested in Jung's typology, though not necessarily in Jung. It was inevitable that in working on this book, I would be immediately confronted with a psychological phenomenon in its own right, namely the Myers-Briggs Type Indicator®. In part, because of this typological testing instrument, droves of people who were otherwise uninterested or uninformed about Jung's psychology were being exposed to and excited by a version of his typology that has become immensely influential and popular.

Another intention then behind the original book became to provide a bridge back to Jung's general psychological model for those people who were already caught by Jung's typology via the MBTI®.

Not too much has changed since. The MBTI contingent continues to grow as a psychological phenomenon, pressing many individuals connected to the MBTI to guard more and more against the trivialization and misuse of their instrument. These individuals are in fact looking for more depth and insight by going back to the source, i.e., Jung's psychology proper.

The resurgence of interest in Jung's model and psychological vision also continues. With best sellers such as Joseph Campbell's *The Power of Myth*, Robert Bly's *Iron John*, Thomas Moore's *Care of the Soul*, and Clarissa Pinkola Estés' *Women Who Run with the Wolves*, more people than ever are interested in Jung's work, looking for ways to get into it without being unduly intimidated. Some of those individuals may find that the attention they give to Jung's typology can be as equally rewarding as his more imagistic, mythological studies that are at the source of such popular works listed above. Typology in fact is an excellent complement to the more imagistic, archetypal works that Jung's psychology is known to have inspired.

For this edition I have made some important additions and revisions as well as added a chapter on "Type Development and the Individuation Process." The additions and revisions are few but significant, two of which deserve note. In Chapter I, I have provided more historical context to help the reader get a sense of how and why typology emerged as a major obsession in Jung's own life. It was important for me to do this to afford balance to the often too bright and "cheery" sense that people take from Jung's typological work.

Chapter VI, "Type Development and the Individuation Process," has been added to the original manuscript. I hasten to say, however, that this chapter is largely speculative. I have had the benefit of studying *Analytical Psychology, the Seminar Given in 1925*, which was not available to me earlier and which I believe provides some important clues on outlining developmental theory for Jung's typology. I also continue to use typology in my clinical work with clients, which affords me some general insight concerning type development and the individuation process. But none of this wholly recommends what I have to say in this chapter.

Essentially, I am responding in this chapter out of what I believe to be a felt need on the part of those interested in Jung's typology. In the past dozen years of presenting lectures and doing workshops on Jung's typology, one of the more pressing issues seemed to be that of conceptualizing type development and relating it to the individuation process. What I have to say is offered along those lines, as something to scratch against, be annoyed by, and maybe eventually to refine and make acceptable.

Preface to the First Edition

CAN A PSYCHOLOGICAL THEORY have a symptomatology? Quirks and spasms? Sweats and shakes? For some time now, something like that has been going on with Jungian typology, and the situation seems to be getting more intense. The current paroxysm of activity around Jung's theory on psychological types is out of place, extreme, ebullient. After all, Jung's theory is over seventy years old; things should be slowing down.

Or are these symptoms in the eye of this beholder? Perhaps instead the theory is coming into its own. Perhaps it has grown wiser and more dignified with age, and so more influential. Is it possible that a theory can individuate?

In Chapter I, I provide a Jungian explanation for a phenomenon I call "typological frenzy," a phenomenon best represented by the incredible growth in activity around a Jungian-based typological testing instrument called the Myers-Briggs Type Indicator® (MBTI®). For some years now, the MBTI has had much to do with increased public interest in Jung's typology. Promotional material for the MBTI dated for the year 1983 informs us that over 750,000 typological indicators were administered, scored, and interpreted. In 1993, that number is reported to have increased to three million.

Presumably a good number of the individuals who disseminate typological information relating to the MBTI belong to the Association for Psychological Type (APT). That organization has increased its membership from 1,700 individuals in 1983 to 7,200 individuals in 1993. Membership in the organization includes individuals from a wide range of professions among which the mental health fields figure prominently, but by no means exclusively.

The dramatic increase in numbers over the last ten years

in regard to both the circulation of Indicators in the general public as well as the small army that has developed around the Indicator's varied applications is certainly a significant psychological fact that warrants its own treatment. Furthermore, when one considers the current 12 to 1 ratio that characterizes the relationship of APT members to Jungian analysts in the United States, one is inclined to wonder who is doing what to whom with Jungian typology.

My point in Chapter I and a central theme throughout the book is that Jungian typology has gone beyond the personal and is triggering something in the collective unconscious. A safe prediction for the future is that one can expect to see more and more "typologies," Jungian-based and otherwise, hitting the commercial market. If nothing else, mere good consumerism demands added perspective.

In Chapter II, I present a summary of Jung's typological theory from his book on psychological types. People familiar with Jung's writings have at times complained that he was not a systematic thinker. Perhaps not. Yet when it came to his writing, this Swiss author was certainly more organized than many of his future readers. In particular, his book *Psychological Types* demonstrates a clarity and structure which is characteristic of a person who has thought long and hard about what he wanted to say, and has gone on to say it.

As in all provocative texts, there will be necessary ambivalence and room for conflicting interpretations. Jung's *Psychological Types* in this sense contains a few theoretical knots that must be accounted for in our study. But considering the complexity and range of the subject matter with which Jung is dealing, these "knots" more often than not serve to enhance one's appreciation for Jung's overall efforts and insights.

In Chapter III, I put typological theory to the test. This chapter is perhaps the most idiosyncratic in the book. I begin with the intention of using typology to delineate Jung's own psychological type. But en route to that goal I make a somewhat eccentric excursus into how one would ideally apply typology in any context. A consequence of this diversion is what may be thought of as a loose set of guidelines on how to effectively and properly use typology. After these typological "guidelines" are in place, I posit Jung's own psychological type and set up a dialogue between, fittingly, "Jung" and his counter-type or typological opposite, a personage I call "Jabbok." The dialogue serves several purposes consistent with the main intentions in Chapter III, as well as preparing the reader for Chapter IV.

Chapter IV is a special treatment of the troublesome fourth function in typological theory. By representing the dark side of a person's psychological type, the inferior function presents the individual with problems usually fought out on the periphery of consciousness. This ends up making the inferior function a demanding moral issue in its own right, often dramatizing deep and serious conflicts between the person's conscious and unconscious life, conflicts which beg for resolution or integration. Without question, the inferior function is the most challenging aspect of Jung's typological theory, and is therefore treated in this chapter with the seriousness it properly deserves.

Because of problems raised in dealing with the inferior function in Chapter IV, it was necessary in Chapter V to tie in closer to Jung's larger psychological model, a model that deals more specifically and deliberately with the unconscious than does his typology per se. *Psychological Types* depicts the various ego patterns available to the personality and conveys a rich and detailed picture of the psyche from the point of view of ego-consciousness. While one can use typology exclusively as a psychology of consciousness at the expense of any realization of the unconscious, this was clearly not Jung's intention. In this chapter, I therefore try to make clear the connections between typology and Jungian psychology proper.

The last section in Chapter V is a brief introduction to what Jung refers to as "the transcendent function." The transcendent function may be thought of as the fifth or quintessential function that is at the heart of the collaborative effort made between consciousness and the unconscious. The transcendent function therefore provides a creative link between typology and some of the larger analytical issues that Jung is concerned to treat in his psychology.

In the Conclusion, I keep a promise made in Chapter I: to provide a corrective to the creative misreadings that Jung's book on psychological types seems to inspire. My means here is a retelling of "The Homeric Hymn to Hermes" as it may pertain to Jung's intentions in coming up with and applying his typology.

Two appendices are included to treat the relative theoretical contributions made to Jungian typology by two practical tools used in typological research: the earlier mentioned Myers-Briggs Type Indicator (MBTI) and the Singer-Loomis Inventory of Personality (SLIP). Both typological tests embody significant theoretical innovations which are worthy of consideration by anyone interested in Jung's original work on psychological types.

A popular subject such as Jungian typology can prove to be one's ruin. With all the activity taking place around Jungian typology, it now becomes easy to view the energy at the source of Jung's original efforts to be somehow dissipating, the focus of the work going blurry or spreading thin. I have written this book intending to stay close to the source, keeping the energy high and the focus clear. My hope is that when "typological frenzy" passes, this little work on typology will still be around to help guide one through the splendid labyrinth of Jung's works, for which typology itself can serve as Ariadne's thread.

Acknowledgments

SPECIAL THANKS go to the following people: to my sister, Dr. Mary Theresa Spoto, whose insight and sensitivity on literary matters continue to be everywhere on the mark.

Drs. Clay McNearney, Nancy Struever, Ken Carter, and Rose Frank contributed in direct and indirect ways to my interest in Jung. Interestingly, none of these individuals would dare think of themselves as "Jungian."

My friend Jim Johnston graciously spent chunks of several weekends bringing the diagrams up to par.

Randy Cooper and Yung Leung used their computer skills and time compiling the index.

At several major junctions in the course of completing this book, my parents, Angelo and Lily, gave of their time, energy, and love. Their presence in the book of my life has been equally valuable.

My six-year-old son, Alex, has been my paradigm for curiosity, vitality, and overall *joie de vivre*.

My wife, Elora, continues to be my supportive, insightful, and challenging partner-in-life. Her own measure of security and strength makes whatever good work I do possible.

Citations and Notes

THE ABBREVIATION "CW" throughout our text refers to *The Collected Works of C. G. Jung* (H. Read, M. Fordham, G. Adler, and W. McGuire, eds.; R. F. C. Hull, trans.), Princeton: Princeton University Press, Bollingen Series XX, vols. 1–20. Where possible, these works are cited by volume number and paragraph number, as in CW 7, para. 268.

Endnotes are found at the end of each chapter rather than grouped at the end of the book.

An Introduction to Jungian Typology

IN THE COURSE of this study, "Jungian typology" will refer to a specific method of careful observation of similarities and differences among individual personalities in the everyday world. These similarities and differences are in turn grouped according to certain formal principles elaborated by C. G. Jung which lead to an understanding of what he terms "psychological types." By helping to identify certain patterns of characteristic behaviors, Jungian typology can be utilized for purposes of study, therapy, and self-understanding. Jungian typology is a theory.

I

Jung's Typology:
Then and Now

Theories in psychology are the very devil.

(CW 17, Foreword, p. 7)

TO APPROACH AND USE JUNG'S typological theory effectively, it's important to get a sense of how it emerged from Jung's own life struggle and where it fits into Jung's psychology as a whole. Typology has its roots in conflict and opposition, experienced both internally and externally for Jung in poignant and often compelling ways. Typology, in a sense, culminates one of the darkest periods in Jung's own development. This period, from about 1913–1919, was referred to by Jung himself as his "confrontation with the unconscious" (Jung, 1973, pp. 170–199). It is also referred to by the editors of the *Collected Works* as Jung's "fallow period," a period of intense self-absorption in which no "real" work was accomplished. Henri Ellenberger, in his classic work *The Discovery of the Unconscious*, describes the time for Jung more provocatively as a period of "creative illness."

Especially during the first eighteen months of this period, Jung was devoting his attention to experimenting with

and carefully observing and documenting his own psychological processes. This included practicing various psychological exercises and different intrapsychic techniques,
searching through childhood memories, playing and working in different media, and largely being open to whatever
emotions, images, and forms the unconscious had to offer
him. From the outside looking in, it probably did appear that
at times Jung had gone off the deep end, or was in effect
"ill." And, in truth, Jung himself no doubt was vulnerable to
what was occurring in regard to his relationship with the
unconscious. There are definite risks in involving oneself in
what Ellenberger goes on to describe as "an intense preoccu-
pation with the mysteries of the human soul" (Ellenberger,
1970, p. 672).

Still, Jung himself had no doubt about the importance of
this time for his own personal psychology and the course of
his future work. His comments in his autobiography, *Memories, Dreams, Reflections*, are unequivocal:

> The years when I was pursuing my inner images were the
> most important in my life—in them everything essential
> was decided. It all began then; the later details are only sup-
> plements and clarifications of the material that burst forth
> from the unconscious, and at first swamped me. It was the
> *prima materia* for a lifetime's work. (Jung, 1973, p. 199)

In his "confrontation," Jung had, in effect, been in touch
with, encountered, the raw essence of his life and life's work
and found in this encounter his destiny, his myth, and his
meaning.

Part of what threw Jung into this intense and emotional
period was his dramatic separation from Freud in 1913.
Because, as we will see, typology is connected with Jung's
relationship to Freud, it is important to know something
about what was going on between these two giants in the
field.

Freud and Jung met for the first time in February of 1907.
The meeting had quite a buildup. During Jung's early days at
the Burghölzli Clinic (1902–1909), he was working in earnest
on the word association experiments, seeking to scientifically document the existence of what he termed "complexes" in

the unconscious. Complexes were understood as emotionally charged configurations of psychic energy characterized by associated images and ideas and capable of living a life of their own, hidden away from the individual's immediate awareness. As such, complexes were also liable to interfere, encroach, and falsify everyday consciousness, getting the person into all sorts of problems and confusions.

Jung's work with the word association test was proof for him that consciousness itself was the proverbial "tip of the iceberg." Consciousness was, in effect, surrounded, afloat, and, in significant ways, at the mercy of the deep, blue, and largely unchartered waters of the unconscious, waters full of alternative life, i.e., the complexes.

These experimental researches of Jung's overlapped nicely with Freud's own preoccupations with the unseen and repressive forces thought by him to shape personality. It would appear to Freud that he had found in Jung a young and ambitious medical doctor involved in research at an internationally renowned psychiatric hospital, an able and influential representative outside his own incestuous Vienna circle. Jung, in effect, could give Freud's movement greater credibility, breadth, and objectivity.

In Jung's mind, the relationship with Freud could be equally useful and important. Freud was someone whom Jung found to be on the cutting edge of psychology, exactly where everyone in the field should be going, and certainly where Jung himself saw his own work heading. He was also, by Jung's account, "the first man of real importance I had encountered" (Jung, 1973, p. 149). Jung would even later confess to having something of a "religious crush" on Freud.

By the time then that Freud and Jung met in Vienna at Freud's apartment, the two men were primed for a fateful encounter. In the passion of that incredible historical moment, Freud and Jung joined forces, joined psyches, and for the next few years, Jung's personal and professional identity would in some way be hooked problematically into Freud's and the psychoanalytic movement.

It was a difficult alliance even from the beginning. Freud, at fifty-one years of age, probably knew this as well as Jung did at thirty-two years. But, they more or less served each other's needs for the next five years.

Theoretically speaking, it was with the two-part publication in 1911 and 1912 of Jung's study on *libido* (first entitled *Psychology of the Unconscious*, later retitled as *Symbols of Transformation* [CW 5]) that Jung finally had drawn the lines of battle between the Vienna and Zürich schools. The differences and oppositions between the two camps were from then on indeed pronounced. Jung could no longer indulge Freud's understanding of libido as tied exclusively to Freud's theory of sexuality. He would argue aggressively in part two of this work that libido is better understood not as sexual energy, a la Freud, but rather more generally as *psychic* energy. As such, libido was capable of being taken up in virtually endless transformations, sexuality being simply one of those formations. Professionally, Jung in effect accused Freud of reducing the structure and processes of the unconscious to Freud's own neurotic bias toward sexuality. Personally, this was tantamount to putting a bullet in Freud's head. This move on Jung's part could not and would not be forgiven by Freud.

When one reads the Freud/Jung correspondence, it is relatively easy to get the sense that their break was in some tragic way inevitable. Jung's famous letter of January 6, 1912, puts the event in Shakespearean form:

> Dear Professor Freud,
>
> I shall submit to your wish to discontinue our personal relationship, for I never force my friendship on anyone. For the rest, you yourself know best what this moment means to you. "The rest is silence . . . "
>
> Yours sincerely,
>
> Jung

Conflict and dissension were characteristic of the psychoanalytic movement as a whole. Alfred Adler had already defected from Freud's following, shaping his own model in hostile opposition to Freud. Now, Jung, at one time considered to be the heir apparent to Freud's psychoanalytic kingdom, found himself with Adler on the other side of the tracks.

That, however, was hardly any consolation for Jung. Adler too, from Jung's perspective, was reductionistic, trying like

Freud to simplify the psyche according to one basic theory or principle. In Adler's case this principle was the need to be superior.

For Jung, while both Freud's and Adler's theories were "true," given their respective assumptions, either one or both together were not true enough to the complexity of the task at hand as Jung understood it. That is, Freud's and Adler's theories did not do justice to the mystery and complexity of the psyche as Jung knew and experienced it. For Jung the variety of contents in the unconscious that he himself was encountering with his patients at the clinic as well as in his own life was being explained away by Freud and Adler, and in this sense both Freud and Adler revealed a disrespectful attitude to the psyche as a whole.

Now, what, you may ask, does all this furor have to do with typology? These conflicts and oppositions with Freud and Adler played directly into Jung's "creative illness," forcing Jung during his confrontation with the unconscious to confront not only the images from his unconscious but the presumptions of consciousness as well. That is, part of Jung's struggle involved taking account of his own ideas, especially in opposition to Freud and Adler. This meant in turn viewing Jung's own life and work, along with Freud's and Adler's, in a "typological" context.

Psychological theory, Jung realized, was innately subjective, a "confession" of consciousness, representing different typological biases on the part of theorists who promoted them. The first order of business for Jung, then, seemed to be to understand the different forms that consciousness could take and how these forms operated within the individual and in the world.

It was all of the problems within the psychoanalytic movement—the issues of differences, conflict, and oppositions—that forced Jung more and more diligently into his typological studies, and in turn gave him motivation to better understand his own typological biases, perhaps even to avoid making the same reductionistic errors Freud and Adler had made.

We get a sense of the importance of typology for Jung when, in 1914, in the heart of his confrontation with the unconscious, Jung addresses the Psycho-Medical Society of

London saying, "the type question is one of the most vital for our psychology and any further advance will probably be along those lines" (CW 3, para. 419). Even earlier, in 1913 in an essay entitled "Contributions to the Study of Psychological Types" (CW 6, Appendix 1), Jung had already outlined what a book on types could look like.

By 1921 the massive volume *Psychological Types* was out. It was Jung's delineation and response to the "type problem" as he knew and experienced it firsthand. Significantly, this first major work to come out of Jung's "confrontation of the unconscious" would be what he termed his "psychology of consciousness."

In coming to terms with his own life after the break with Freud, Jung was in a very real way alone with his own psychology, i.e., the emotions, images, and ideas of Jung the man. One end of his work would eventually culminate in Jung's career years later in his studies on alchemy. There the focus would be on developing the connections between his work with the unconscious and the work of the alchemists as a historical and psychological analog to his own evolving psychological model.

However, equally important during this time, and perhaps even of more *immediate* significance, was the work Jung was doing on himself to distinguish his own thinking from that of Freud's and Adler's, and in the process fleshing out his understanding of the forms of consciousness and their relationship to the unconscious. This was his typological project.

Being thrown into a period of total disorientation, and inner and outer conflict, forced the problems of differences and opposites onto Jung in vitally urgent ways, ultimately resulting in the publication of *Psychological Types,* one of Jung's major works.

Not a few Jungian analysts generally balk at this work, finding it too cumbersome or inhibiting in the analytic process. But, in the years to come, Jung would never abandon his theory of typology. He would, in effect, build a larger context in which typology could be successfully and usefully integrated and absorbed.

In order to follow the thread of Jung's typological work throughout Jung's career, it is helpful and important now to draw a distinction between the problem of differences and the problem of opposites in Jung's book *Psychological Types.* The problem of differences has been taken up with a vengeance by advocates and users of the incredibly popular typological assessment tool called the Myers-Briggs Type Indicator, of which I will have much more to say shortly. My concern here is that some of the heat and passion that Jung originally experienced during the time of writing *Psychological Types* may be getting lost if all we focus on in typology is the problem of differences. The problem of differences was certainly on Jung's mind at this critical time in his life. But it is easy to exalt the problem of differences at the expense of the problem of opposites. For Jung typology has at its core the experience of the intrapsychic and interpsychic conflict, manifesting through what is better understood as the problem of opposites.

This is not simply a semantic squabble. The problem of opposites includes the problem of differences, but dramatically emphasizes the conflict and tension between conscious and unconscious life, precisely what Jung was experiencing during his confrontation with the unconscious. When Jung is speaking on the problem of opposites, he always expresses himself with great passion, strength, and insight. In fact, the problem of opposites is what will remain an obsession for Jung throughout his life. The problem of opposites, then, needs to be untangled from the problem of differences, the former being Jung's driving concern and what gives life to the problem of differences. In the foreword to the Argentine edition of *Psychological Types* (1934), Jung tells us as much when he states,

> I would recommend the reader who really wants to understand my book to immerse himself first of all in chapters II and V. He will gain more from them than from any typological terminology superficially picked up, since this serves no other purpose than a totally useless desire to stick on labels.

Chapters II and V are the chapters in which Jung tackles the problem of opposites most insightfully.

Some further context for understanding the MBTI movement, with its emphasis on the problem of differences, is

now necessary. Many people who will read this book are
users of the MBTI and will approach this book with an eye to
deepening their understanding of Jung's original work. Spend-
ing some time connecting to the MBTI community is well
worth the effort.

＊＊＊＊＊

In June of 1987, the Association of Psychological Type (APT)
held its seventh biennial international conference in
Gainesville, Florida. An APT promotional flier published in
1987 stated that in 1979 this "national membership was
formed to bring people and type information together
through publications, local, regional, and national conferences and the APT Training Program." For their annual paid
membership fee, members then received *The Bulletin of Psychological Type* three times a year, which contained current
articles, reports, and book reviews on a variety of applications of psychological type, as well as *The Journal of Psychological Type*, a national research journal published twice a
year, and a national membership directory for networking
purposes, published annually. Services from APT even then
reflected a strong and active membership.

The small college city of Gainesville, Florida, was more
than a coincidental host city for the conference, for then it
was the home of APT as well as the Center for Applications
of Psychological Type, Inc. (CAPT). A CAPT promotional
flier published in 1987 explained that it was founded in 1969
when Isabel Briggs Myers, creator of a Jungian-based typological assessment tool called the Myers-Briggs Type Indicator
(MBTI), began a collaboration with Mary McCaulley, a clinical psychologist at the University of Florida. At the time of
this writing the Center's mission statement reads as follows:

> CAPT's mission is to extend and teach the accurate under-
> standing and the clinical and practical applications of Jung's
> theory of psychological types, which shows how our differ-
> ences in experiencing events and making decisions can be
> valuable rather than divisive, and can be used constructive-
> ly to promote personal development, to manage conflict,
> and to increase human understanding worldwide.

The rapid growth of CAPT in recent years is especially noteworthy since it seems to be animated by a spirit marked by nothing less than missionary zeal among many of its members. Now, in addition to serving as a research laboratory with computer scoring services and a data bank for over five hundred thousand MBTI results, CAPT distributes a publishing catalog which includes literature on Jungian typology, the Myers-Briggs Type Indicator testing materials, references and bibliographic aids, consulting services, and various materials for trainers using the MBTI in individual and group settings. The CAPT faculty also regularly schedules training workshops on the theory, research, and practical applications of Jungian typology as implemented through the Myers-Briggs Type Indicator.

In the last few years APT and CAPT have combined forces to provide a unique qualifying workshop designed to allow individuals from various academic backgrounds and professions outside psychology to access and use MBTI testing materials for their special purposes. The MBTI is designated a level "B" instrument by its publisher, Consulting Psychologists Press, and normally would be restricted to professionals in psychological fields or individuals who have completed course work in tests and measurements at a university level. But, for all practical purposes, the tool is now available to anyone satisfactorily completing the APT/CAPT qualifying workshop.

No doubt one of the virtues of Jung's theory on psychological types is that to many it seems simple enough to be taught and applied in a variety of contexts. However, this apparent feature of the theory is not without its own share of special problems.

Familiar with Jung's typology and the enterprising efforts of such organizations as APT and CAPT, I was still very much surprised to read some years ago that the consulting firm of Otto Kroeger had been providing a course to the National War College entitled "Executive Skills Development," a course based on Jung's typology as applied through the Myers-Briggs Type Indicator. One of the goals of this course was to develop a particular personality type called an ISTJ (Keen, 1986, p. 82). In Myers-Briggs shorthand an "ISTJ" is a typological designation for an introvert with sensing as a dominant perceiving function who extraverts thinking as an auxiliary judging function, all special terms that will become clear shortly.

The fact that typology is now in the War College is not reason in itself for alarm. What is important for us to note is that Jungian typology is quickly and efficiently being made to work in behalf of anyone or anything, especially with as reliable an instrument as the MBTI to promote Jung's initial findings.

Along these same lines we read in the current MBTI literature that a multitude of companies and organizations are using the MBTI for team building, conflict management, and career development (Hirsch, 1985, p. 1). Here too, one must wonder how often typology may likewise be used by the power structure of such companies to separate the wheat from the chaff in regard to job assignments or hiring, firing, and promotional practices. These latter applications are of course specifically against the ethical standards of both APT and CAPT. However, very few users of the MBTI in organizational settings would not suspect that such practices do indeed exist and perhaps in greater number than MBTI "evangelists" may be willing to admit.

As one might now begin to imagine, Jung's book *Psychological Types* (CW 6), on which all of this often frenzied activity and enterprise is based, seems now unmatched in popular appeal among the twenty volumes of his *Collected Works*. (The *Collected Works* themselves are the most significant part of the critically acclaimed Bollingen Series.[1])

While much of Jung's work is currently going through a remarkable renascence, Jungian typology specifically seems to have earned Jung more interest, credibility, and acceptance among a greater variety of professionals than other equally fertile Jungian formulations, such as the collective unconscious, archetypal psychology, active imagination, synchronicity, and the individuation process.

I am not sure how Jung would have felt about all this. My guess is that he personally would have been critical of or at best concerned about the speed in which his typological theory has been disseminated through the "tests and measurements" approach. At the very least one would suspect that he would have warned us about making too much of typology outside the context and intentions of his work as a whole.

Yet to some degree the popularization of Jungian typology is reminiscent of the times when Jung himself was alive and his influence was being felt through different projects and groups intent on promoting his work. It would be interesting indeed to explore what may be the historical and cultural reasons for all of this "typological activity" occurring primarily here and now in the United States. If, as Toni Wolff once stated, "the history of ideas follows the law of compensation" (1956, p. 11), perhaps we may suspect that the hegemony of behavioristic models is on the wane.

However, for present purposes I want to take a somewhat more modest and personal approach to this growth phenomenon. We will begin by looking at some examples of Jung's influence on people's lives and how that influence often led to collective or organized efforts to further Jung's work. In this regard the first story we can recount has to do with the mother and daughter team that came up with the Myers-Briggs Type Indicator. In many ways it is fitting we begin here, since this psychological instrument has been tied to much of the current contagion of interest in Jung's work.

Isabel Briggs Myers tells the story of her mother, Katharine Briggs, beset with the task of trying to figure out who her daughter had brought home to the family dinner table one Christmas vacation. Apparently, the fellow with whom Isabel had fallen in love was somewhat strange by family standards, and, to make matters worse, it seemed that marriage was in the air.

The mother began a project of reading many and varied biographies, believing she could get some insight into different types of people, perhaps even her soon-to-be son-in-law. As she read, she noted recurring patterns which eventually formed the beginnings of her own typological study. After a certain point in her research, she concluded that there were four types of individuals: the meditative types, the spontaneous types, the executive types, and the sociable types.

Then Katharine Briggs discovered *Psychological Types* and considered it a revelation which she had to share with her daughter Isabel. They both found the book so stimulating and so rich that they began working together on "typological

projects" that would eventually culminate in the now celebrated Myers-Briggs Type Indicator. While a joint venture at
first, the bulk of the actual work for the MBTI would be done
by Isabel Briggs Myers over a twenty-two-year period from
1940 to 1962, the year in which Educational Testing Services
(ETS) published the Research Form F of the MBTI and the
first MBTI manual.

It should be noted that the tenacity and purposefulness
which Isabel Briggs Myers expressed in seeing her dream
through to such a successful end was spurred on by her belief
that typology, if used properly, could enhance the efficiency
of people working together during World War II. At the out-
break of the war, she felt that a properly developed typological assessment tool could be used to better match personalities and talents to complete those jobs necessary to bring the
war effort to a quick and successful conclusion (McCaulley,
1980, pp. 2–5). Kroeger's aforementioned efforts at the War
College may actually be a variation on this theme. Nonetheless, the down-to-earth early concerns of mother and daughter trying to "figure out" this new would-be family member
seemed to have been their shared, significant, and sincere
motivations for working with Jung's book in the first place.

Such personal and global motivations behind the story of
the development of the MBTI also make the historical evolution of the instrument an excellent indication of the attraction that Jungian typology has for many people, as well as a
sign of the devotion to ideas which Jung's work as a whole is
capable of inspiring. Since her death in 1980 at the age of
eighty-two, a reverent following has built up around the
memory and accomplishment of "Isabel" herself, as Isabel
Briggs Myers is affectionately remembered by many of her
successors. Yet I believe that this very idealistic and determined woman would be the first to acknowledge that Jung's
writings (especially, of course, his work on psychological
types) were at the heart of her life and work.

Today, it is not unusual to find people who have read
parts of *Psychological Types* and who can describe particular
situations in their lives which begged for some perspective or
ordering that Jung's book seemed to provide. I have known
individuals who have chronicled broken relationships, lost
jobs, and family battles in the margins of the text, almost in

exchange for the larger insights and motivations which the book was able to offer them at those critical times in their lives.

What came across in Jung's written works was especially obvious to those around him when he was alive. Jung seemed to inspire a following who utilized his work to explore their own individual lives as well as to carry on group activities having to do with what may be called the psychology of the planet. These aspects of Jung's work and influence no doubt have made for various and eccentric epigoni. But these same aspects make much of what comes out of a Jungian framework unusually provocative and wide-ranging.

The personal effect Jung had on people is probably best summarized in Barbara Hannah's comment early in her biographical memoir of Jung. After reading Jung's works and attending his lectures and seminars, Hannah was determined to get closer to Jung the man. Soon after first coming to know him on a more personal basis, she remarks, " . . . he was already living the psychology that would make him famous . . . The really convincing thing was Jung himself. He was his own psychology" (1976, p. 31).

Jung seemed to embody in his own personality the insights which his psychology sought to describe and explain for others in the larger context of events. Because Jung's own vision was so broad and deep, people who knew him developed an extraordinary sense that the work he was doing for himself actually tied creatively into their own lives and to greater humanity as well.

This "numinous" aspect of Jung's personality is still quite alive today, even among the third generation Jungians who often wish to identify themselves as going against or beyond the traditions of "the old master." There is no scarcity of available biographies of Jung to both illustrate and critique these aspects of the "Jung legend" (Hannah, 1976; von Franz, 1975; van der Post, 1975; Brome, 1978; Jaffé, 1979; Wehr, 1971, 1987; Stern, 1976; Bennet, 1962; Homans, 1979; Rolfe, 1989; Kerr, 1993).

In reading many of Jung's biographies, I am also struck by all the movement, deliberation, and influence that collected around a person who described his own life as "singularly poor in outward happenings" (Jung, 1973, p. 5). For the major portion of his life, Jung often had brilliant, productive, and fiercely loyal people working closely with him, persons such as Marie-Louise von Franz, Barbara Hannah, Esther Harding, Jolande Jacobi, Eleanor Bertine, and Aniela Jaffé, to mention only some of the more notable and accomplished women. This is not to mention all the talented and accomplished "outsiders" in other fields and walks of life who kept up with or played into what Jung himself was producing. The biographies together make clear that whatever and whomever Jung struggled with in the first half of his life, he was certainly not lacking in intellectual, financial, or organizational backing during the second half of his life.

From this biographical material I have chosen two examples to illustrate how collective efforts have arisen from individuals influenced by Jung. The first has to do with Jung's participation in the annual Eranos conferences, and the second has to do with the development and establishment of the Jung Institutes around the world.

The Eranos conferences (*eranos* = "shared feast"), initiated by Olga Froebe-Kapteyn, were meetings held annually in Ascona, Switzerland, whose purpose was to collect outstanding representatives from various disciplines and provide a centering point for the give-and-take of ideas, especially as those ideas connected the intellectual traditions of the East and West. The conferences had been going on a couple of years before Jung was first invited to speak, yet his participation commanded such attention—and he personally was so often at the center of discussions—that Froebe-Kapteyn came to speak of the conferences as having begun in 1933, the year of Jung's first presentation (Hannah, 1976, pp. 215–216).

Marie-Louise von Franz described these annual gatherings as "broad humanistic and scientific discussions on a very high level" (1975, p. 127). Even that may be an understatement. While Jung attended the conferences more or less regularly from 1933 until 1953, he presented papers with the likes of Karl Kerényi (mythology), Henry Corbin (Persian mysticism), Adolf Portman (biology), Hugo Rahner (Christian symbolism), Gershom Scholem (Jewish mysticism), Sir Herbert Read (art history), Mircea Eliade (history of religion, anthropology), Heinrich Zimmer (Indian philosophy), Martin Buber (theology), Walter Otto (classical studies), Victor White (theology), Erich Neumann (psychology), Karl Löwith (history), D. T. Suzuki (Zen Buddhism), and Paul Tillich (theology), among others (Campbell, 1969, pp. 376–388). The cross-fertilization of ideas and the charged atmosphere at these conferences during this period must have been awe-inspiring (Jaffé, 1977, pp. 201–212.)

If one looks at the topics under discussion after Jung's death in 1961 (the conferences have continued), almost all seem to be on what could properly be called Jungian topics or Jungian related concerns. In fact, a collection of pictures on religious art and archaeology which illustrates the archetypal themes discussed at the yearly Eranos conferences was started by none other that Olga Froebe-Kapteyn herself, and was further developed after Jung's death eventually becoming the Archive for Research in Archetypal Symbolism (ARAS), currently housed at the C. G. Jung Institute in New York, with duplicate copies at the San Francisco and Los Angeles Institutes (Henderson, 1982, p. 14).

I, of course, am not suggesting that the likes of such seminal thinkers as listed above were working for or even specifically with Jung. Rather, I am drawing attention to the fact that Jung was surrounded by the good and credible efforts of talented people who in their own right accomplished work that seemed to advance Jung's own larger concerns. Some, like Olga Froebe-Kapteyn, did this in a very direct manner through organizing the Eranos conferences and compiling research on archetypal symbols. Others, like many of the Eranos participants, did so more indirectly by connecting with Jung at their own levels of expertise.

Not inconsistent with his introversion on matters of this kind, Jung himself was determined not to draw any extra attention to himself or his psychology during the conferences. Yet the law of intellectual gravity operating at Eranos often worked to the contrary, pulling conference participants and topics to Jung himself, which is to say to Jungian psychology (Jaffé, 1977).

The second and more specific instance of Jung's extended presence manifested through a collective effort has to do with the formation of the Jung Institutes themselves, dating from the first Psychological Club formed in Zürich in 1916. As another indication of the widespread support for Jung's work, I will simply mention as an aside that Jung was initially assisted in the funding and organization of the Psychological Club by Edith McCormick, the daughter of John D. Rockefeller and wife of Harold McCormick (Hannah, 1976, p. 130). For our purposes the main consideration is that the club was formed, in Barbara Hannah's words, "to give the group of people that were increasingly gathering around Jung some sense of corporate life" (Ibid.).

The Psychological Club had been in existence for twenty-nine years as a place where pupils and patients of Jung could meet and exchange views, share companionship, and participate in lectures on matters relating to analytical psychology. Then, in 1945, on the occasion of Jung's seventieth birthday, Dr. Jolande Jacobi began to stir up interest among several members of the Psychological Club to found an institute in Jung's name. Primarily due to health problems, Jung was not ready to begin the institute when Jacobi proposed it. However, two years later in 1947 he surprised many at a Psychological Club meeting when he himself proposed its foundation. Everyone present at the meeting was delighted and immediately rallied their full support.

Jung Institutes now exist in Zürich, London, Berlin, Tel Aviv, Paris, Sao Paolo, Rome, Brussels, Stuttgart, New York, Chicago, Dallas, Boston, Los Angeles, and San Francisco. At any of these locations, the requirements for certification as a "Jungian analyst" are intense and difficult. Most institutes have a six-year program which includes a minimum of three hundred hours of personal analysis for the trainee, continuous course work in analytical psychology, and ongoing clinical supervision.

An excellent article entitled "The Education of the Analyst" by Jungian analyst June Singer (1982) summarizes the various aspects of the process that constitute most Jungian analysts' life work.

* Analysts act as companions to the soul on its path.
* Analysts recognize a responsibility to the entire organism.
* Analysts recognize developmental patterns.
* Analysts recognize typological differences among individuals.

*Analysts help to bring into sharp focus the unique individuality of the person.
*Analysts ally themselves with the creative potential of the analysands.
*Analysts seek to provide a solid reference point in ordinary reality.
*Analysts look for the purposive dynamism of the psyche.
*Analysts carefully note the transference-countertransference aspects of the analytical encounter.

Singer suggests here that Jung "the legend" has been displaced in favor of a Jungian approach to the therapeutic situation. She also implies that the best of what comes out of the Jung Institutes can do much to assuage Jung's own apprehension concerning the many imitators who collected around him during his lifetime. If Singer's words are any true sign of the legacy which Jung left to the Institutes, one may believe that Jung's efforts have been richly rewarded—all this from a man who complained midway in his career, "Thank God I am Jung, and not a Jungian" (Hannah, 1976, p. 78).

We have implied that the resurgence of interest in and study of Jungian typology seems to have a certain personal effect on individuals, which often makes itself felt in collective or group activity. This phenomenon seems to be running a parallel course to the "Jung legend," at least in regard to the amount of movement and activity Jung's typological theory continues to generate.

When looking at the activity surrounding Jung's life and work, especially in the instances cited above, we may believe equally positive things would come from all the energy being spent on typology. However, the verdict is still out concerning the recent and specific emphasis on Jungian typology via such organizations as APT and CAPT which are, incidentally, among the most responsible agents of Jungian typology in a truly hybrid field of users.

In the United States typological activity has taken an often distasteful commercial turn. Typological "paraphernalia" (coffee mugs, games, tie tacks, posters, type-shirts, badges, etc.) have sprung up at typological conferences, and at least one type-oriented television show has been commercially marketed and broadcast on the West Coast. Current marketing of various applications which use typology in business, educational, and religious settings has all but reached the saturation point.

Also, people using typological terminology often express a too easy familiarity with one another in interpersonal exchanges, giving the "outsider" to typology the sense that he or she is being kept out of church for not knowing the catechism. Interestingly enough, in a popular film on Jung's life (*A Matter of Heart*, 1985), analyst Hilde Kirsch comments on her own analysis with Jung by saying that "[Jung] would never use any of his terms, ever." While this comment did apply specifically to Kirsch's own analysis, one suspects that Jung's own use of typological terminology was in other contexts both judicious and restrained.

To put our story so far into some perspective, and to point us in the right direction for our own approach to Jungian typology, I will introduce the Jungian concept of the "archetype," a word common enough to most of us, but with special significance in Jung's psychology.

In Jungian psychology, archetypes are transhistorical or universal psychic tendencies which are not representable in and of themselves, but which are manifested in outer behaviors, symbolic forms, patterns, or images. There is no telling how many archetypes exist, but they all share characteristics that are best thought of as primordial and collective in nature. According to the British analyst and author Andrew Samuels, "archetypal patterns wait to be realized in the personality, are capable of infinite variation, are dependent upon individual expression and exercise a fascination reinforced by traditional or cultural expectation" (1986, p. 26).

Early in Jung's career, Jung referred to the archetype as a "mnemic deposit, an imprint or engram, which has arisen through the condensation of countless processes of a similar kind. In this respect it is a precipitate and, therefore, a typical basic form of certain ever-recurring psychic experiences" (CW 6, para. 748). He would go on to refer to archetypes as "a priori categories of experience," "dominants of the unconscious," and "self-portraits of the instincts," among other phrases.

Archetypes often seem most recognizable in those outer behaviors that cluster around transition states, crises, or universal experiences: birth, marriage, war, motherhood, separation, betrayal, death, and so on. But they should not be thought of as restricted in their effects. The archetypes can have an ineluctable role in the way an individual lives his or her everyday life as well.

If the concept of "archetypes" sounds difficult to understand and get a handle on, it is because it is. James Hillman (1983), a prominent Jungian analyst, has developed a field of inquiry alongside analytical psychology, called archetypal psychology, to identity, unravel, and otherwise come to terms with what Jung has also called "primordial images expressing the psychic situation as a whole" (CW 6, para. 747).

I am bringing up this central Jungian concept now to put it to some use in the more particular topic of "typological frenzy." After studying Jung's typological theory, witnessing firsthand the recent growth of interest in the theory, and researching Jung's life and work, I believe this supremely psychological formulation of Jung's can provide an insight into some of the excesses which seem to come from many individuals currently fascinated by Jung's typology.

Jung and his work constellate for many people what we may term the archetype of "order," an archetype perhaps best represented by the figure of Apollo. At the unconscious level, at certain times and under certain conditions, there arises a universal need to give conscious expression to those characteristics once personified in Greek culture by the god Apollo. I am thinking specifically of Apollo's attributes of form, proportion, clarity, and harmony, his oracle's enigmatic injunction at Delphi to "know yourself," his ability to be "on target" with his bow, and his power with the Muses.

Jung's work generally can make these qualities seem necessary and desirable. But *Psychological Types*, perhaps the most familiar and orderly of his works, is especially evocative in this regard. Jung did not intend this book to come off one-sidedly in favor of what we are calling the archetype of order, and he would have warned of the risks in approaching any of his works in too "orderly" a fashion. Nonetheless, much as Beethoven's Pastoral Symphony followed his conflicted Fifth Symphony, this sixth volume of Jung's *Collected Works* seems to follow the seething and disorderly fifth volume, *Symbols of Transformation*, and has the effect of "putting things in place." Coincidentally, as the Fifth Symphony stylistically marks Beethoven's "break" with Mozart, volume 5 in Jung's works formally marks his painful break with Freud.

Because the archetype of order seems to have played such an important role in both the writing and reading of *Psychological Types*, at the conclusion of our study we will suggest an archetypal "corrective" as a counterweight to this aspect of the text. For now, however, a simple warning about "Apollo" seems important.

Apollo is a formidable and demanding god in his own right, one who will pull a reader's attention toward him if the reader is unaware. In psychological language this would mean that an unconscious consequence of the archetype of order applied to typology will manifest itself in people using Jungian typology to force personality differences into the heuristic concepts or inventions Jung created to explicate his theory. The more its audience needs to have everything fit in a neat and orderly way, the more Jung's work becomes rigid and ossified.

Jung often complained that people misunderstood many of his central concepts by taking them too rigidly or literally. One can certainly see where Jung's typology may be especially vulnerable to such misunderstandings. In the extreme case, used too rigidly or with too "orderly" a purpose, typology can even be thought of as a weapon rather than a tool of understanding. The projected applications of the MBTI during World War II and Kroeger's typology courses for the War College come to mind. Both examples are essentially moral ventures, provided they are conducted at a conscious level.

In the analysis of typology to follow, I will emphasize typology as a "psychology of consciousness." I will also try to maintain a self-critical perspective which an awareness of the historical context can provide, and to emphasize the problem of opposites over and against the problem of differences. But, most importantly, we need to realize that the archetype of order is afoot in both the writing and subsequent readings of Jung's typology. In all these ways I hope to circumvent the "typological frenzy" which sooner or later must run its course, and to reconnect to the main and enduring concerns of Jung's psychology as a whole.

Notes

1. The publication of the Bollingen Series was inaugurated in 1943 as part of a program of the Old Dominion Foundation, which Paul Mellon founded in 1941. In 1945, the Bollingen Foundation was formed as a separate entity to act as the vehicle for publishing the Series as well as a source of funds for fellowships, subventions, and institutional contributions in a variety of humanistic and scientific fields. The Series consists of one hundred numbered publications (over 250 volumes) in fields such as aesthetics, archaeology, cultural history, ethnology, literary criticism, mythology, philosophy, poetry, psychology, religion, and symbolism. In Paul Mellon's words, "The idea of the *Collected Works* of Jung might be considered the central core, the binding factor, not only of the Foundation's general direction but also of the ultimate intellectual temper of the Bollingen Series as a whole." The Bollingen enterprise itself was named for the small village in Switzerland where Jung had built a private retreat (information is from the title page of the 1982 Bollingen Series catalogue, Princeton University Press).

II

Jungian Typology:
A Psychology of Consciousness

It is not the purpose of a psychological typology to classify
human beings into categories; this in itself would be pretty
pointless. Its purpose is to provide a critical psychology which
will make a methodical investigation and presentation of the
empirical material possible.

(CW 6, para. 986)

AT A LECTURE presented at the 1987 APT conference in
Gainesville, Florida and entitled "How a Sensing Type Sur-
vives as a Jungian Analyst," Jungian analyst Mary Ann Mattoon recalled a conversation with C. A. Meier, a close associ-
ate of Jung and a former president of the Jung Institute at
Zürich. Meier reportedly told Mattoon, "the individuation
process begins and ends with typology."

In one sense this was a spectacularly simple statement for
Meier to make, considering how well he knew Jung personally and how careful he would be to present a balanced picture of Jung's work. The "individuation process" which
Meier refers to is after all a key concept in Jung's psychody-
namic theories of personality, and it figures prominently
throughout the *Collected Works*. For the time being, a working definition of "the individuation process" is as follows: "A
person's becoming himself, whole, indivisible and distinct

from other people or collective psychology, though also in relation to these" (Samuels, 1986, p. 76).

After Mattoon's presentation, I had the opportunity to ask her if Meier really meant what he said. She replied to me, "No, of course not."

This is the predicament we are in when we study Jungian typology. By mentioning the quote in her presentation, Mattoon no doubt believed that Meier was saying something quite important about typology. But, she, like Meier, did not want what he said to become important in the wrong way. So she as quickly took the bite out of what both she and Meier said by denying Meier's belief in it at all. This surface irony or gamesmanship is a force to be reckoned with when one is studying Jung or trying to apply his work in everyday settings. Even as straightforward an analyst as Mattoon can be somewhat "tricky," answering a question with an awareness that the underlying issues must be kept open and alive.

Because so much of Jung's work touches the unconscious itself and activates the individual in interesting and sometimes excessive ways, Jungians as a group are guarded about being understood "too well" or providing too many definitive answers. I believe Mattoon was reacting to my question in this typically Jungian manner. Jung himself reportedly told his good friend Laurens van der Post, "Nothing worse could happen to one than to be completely understood" (van der Post, 1975, p. 121).

Jung's comment and Meier's and Mattoon's guile or playfulness have something to do with that much-vaunted and criticized inscrutability for which many Jungians are famous, or perhaps notorious, depending upon one's point of view. Sometimes, however, there is some wisdom in what to many is an irritating insiders' game. In any case, we will come back to Meier's comment later. I do in fact believe that there is much truth to his initial claim.[1]

For now, a better and safer approach with which to begin our study of Jung's typological theory is to give an overview of the structure of Jung's text *Psychological Types*. In the current Bollingen edition (1977), *Psychological Types* is over 550 pages long. The first 330 pages treat what Jung called the "type problem" in a variety of historical, cultural, and philosophical contexts. The question Jung asks himself throughout these sections is whether there are differences among individuals across time and cultures which can be understood or grouped as typical. The answer he comes up with through a dazzling investigation into the history of ideas is an unequivocal "yes."

In this first three-fifths of the book, Jung presents material to substantiate and explain his psychological insights taken from classical and medieval times, into Renaissance and Reformation history, and on to the Enlightenment and nineteenth century philosophical idealism. He also draws liberally from more general disciplines such as modern philosophy, esthetics, poetry, and biography. Nor does he limit himself to Western European cultures. Ample evidence is drawn from Indian, Chinese, and Japanese cultures to make the overall effect of his typological investigations one of broad and rich significance.

The remaining two-fifths of the book are divided into three sections. The first deals formally with detailed type descriptions of different personalities. This is followed by a long section on "definitions," used to support his theory. Finally, the book concludes with an appendix containing four short "position papers," written over a period of twenty-three years, which clarify Jung's purposes in originating a typological theory.

Because Jung's typological theory is based on a particular understanding of polar opposites (which we will go into more fully later), Jung focuses much of his attention on thinkers and historical movements which seem to reflect that often conflicted and paradoxical way of viewing reality. Specifically, when he looks for the type problem in modern philosophy, he quite naturally finds it expressed in William James "tough-minded" and "tender-minded" polarity. In fact, James tabulates for Jung a series of polarities, such as rationalistic-empiricist, intellectualistic-sensationalistic, idealistic-materialistic, optimistic-pessimistic, etc., which became most valuable to Jung in his own psychological typology.

Another example of this methodical approach to historical sources is Jung's review of the nominalism-realism controversy of the Middle Ages, which Jung mines for insights into his own polarity of extraversion-introversion. The "realist" position reflects the introvert's predisposition to see a reality behind the surface (or "naming") of things. This "reality" is taken at the expense of "mere" appearances. The "nominalist" position reflects the extravert's tendency to take at face value what presents itself as "the case," at the expense of looking at what may be invisibly at play behind the scenes.

And, in what nowadays we may call an example of Jungian arcana, Jung even discusses the early Church doctrine of *homoousios* (that Jesus Christ is at once completely God and completely man) as a way to approach the general psychological problem of reconciling opposing attributes in man, specifically what is human and divine in the personality.

The above examples (and Jung's book is full of such illustrations) may seem very much beside the point in a study on psychological differences. But, getting used to Jung's approach to his material and coming to understand the nature of polar oppositions is especially important in coming to terms with Jung's text as a whole.

Another problem facing the modern reader is how wide ranging (some would say exotic or esoteric) Jung's subject matter is. The peculiar combination of overspecialization and cultural illiteracy prevalent these days makes reading Jung's broad and erudite studies a difficult and frustrating task for many otherwise well-intentioned readers. In effect, many people initially drawn to *Psychological Types* end up finding much of Jung's early analysis of the cultural-historical sources too difficult to handle or at best opportunistic or self-justifying on Jung's part. These readers, if they stay with the book at all, end up skipping to the more formal psychological essays in the last third of the book, the section upon which most of the various extensions and applications of Jung's theory are based.

It is unfortunate that most readers will approach Jung this way. Jung is often thought of as dabbling in material that is by traditional psychological standards "off-limits" or inappropriate to the trade. Yet, if one judges Jung's insights on terms slightly more generous and more in keeping with his own intentions, much of this "lost" material would suddenly come alive. In fact, the scholarship in *Psychological Types* is perhaps less susceptible to the charges of idiosyncrasy and fabulation that some of Jung's other works commonly arouse.

Generally with Jung, one finds that the more one reads him, the more one realizes that his intellectual range was exceptionally broad without being superficial.[2] This is one of the reasons many scholars from otherwise competitive disciplines relate well to his work.

As we ourselves are about to leave this scholarly part of Jung's work for the more formal elaboration of his typological theory, I reemphasize that ignoring this difficult and often tedious three-fifths of his book is clearly against the intentions of the author. In this chronological survey of contributions to the "type problem," Jung painstakingly furnishes the reader with enough actual information to inductively experience the psychological lessons and insights which struck Jung so forcefully in his life and subsequent research. This section of the book is thus Jung's way of saying that his theory of psychological types is based on facts psychologically real and already "on the record."

Before we proceed to a formal elaboration of the theory itself, a warning now seems appropriate. One of Jung's favorite Chinese proverbs went like this: "If the wrong man uses the right means, the right means work in the wrong way" (Wilhelm, 1975, p. 79). This could very well apply to the part of *Psychological Types* which we are now about to examine in detail. This section of Jung's book provides "the right means," i.e., the actual theory or method of typology. However, one should not separate the theory or method of typology from the individual using it.

Our study hopes to show that typology properly understood could not allow for such an ethical breach in applications. In other words, one understands typology properly when one is the "proper" individual using it.

The Attitudes

We will now focus on Jungian typology as a method of observing human behavior based on a special understanding and application of the terms extraversion-introversion, thinking-feeling, sensation-intuition. The special nature of this understanding will become clearer as we proceed. For now, a helpful analogy may be drawn between Jungian typology and what has come to be called the "new physics."

As many of the recent books on the new physics convey, physicists are no longer viewing matter as passive or inert, and therefore subject to easy, objective definition and study. Instead, matter itself is viewed metaphorically as a continuous dance whose rhythmic patterns are determined by the molecular, atomic, and nuclear structures of mass interacting with energy.[3]

This dynamic approach to matter and energy is not dissimilar to the one we are going to take in approaching Jung's typological theory. In typology, human behavior is viewed through patterns determined by the structure of the individual's psyche interacting with itself and the world. Because of this reciprocal movement between what is studied and who is doing the studying, we will try in our discussion not simply to establish the terminology, method, and structure of the theory, but to likewise convey the dynamic nature of the reality for which the theory itself was created, i.e., the human personality.

Jung's theory first distinguishes between two very basic typological categories: "attitude-types" and "function-types." In his now-classic formulation of the extraversion-introversion polarity, Jung describes the two attitude types in terms of the direction of libido or orientation of interest (psychic energy)[4] to or away from the object. The second typological category, which Jung calls "function-types," refers to the specific manner or means of adaptation that yields an observable and consciously differentiated psychological "function," or way of dealing with the inner or outer worlds. Jung posits four possible functions: sensation, intuition, thinking, and feeling. Like extraversion-introversion, the functions are connected in polar fashion, thinking-feeling both being described as "rational" or "judging" functions, and sensation-intuition both being described as "irrational" or "perceiving" functions. For the sake of our study, we will examine first the attitude-types and then look at the rational and irrational function-types. This is to some degree setting up an artificial split of the material for purposes of understanding typological theory. Eventually the intention would be to put the attitudes and functions back together to generate a fuller and more dynamic picture of differing psychological types as they manifest in everyday reality.

To begin: Jung believes that the category of extraversion-introversion, as he develops it, reflects typological differences that cross all ranks of society, are gender neutral, and transcend cultural-historical conditions. While Jung states that he will provide only a "broad hint" at the biological justification of the extraversion-introversion polarity, he explicitly expresses his conviction that biological difference is "the actual foundation of our two psychological models" (CW 6, para. 559).

Generally speaking, whenever Jung invokes a biological foundation for his psychological applications (and he does so often), he is alerting the reader to his emphasis on the confrontational aspect of the reality with which he is trying to come to terms. In other words, references to the biological elements playing through typology serve to document psychic realities that cannot be avoided or denied by the individual (Stevens, 1983). In typology, this comes out in how Jung broadly associates the two attitude-types with the manner in which organisms survive or exist in nature. For Jung, any species depends typically upon either "a high rate of fertility, with low powers of defense and short duration of life for the individual organism . . . ," or upon "equipping the individual organism with numerous means of self-preservation plus a low fertility rate" (CW 6, para. 559). In the first case, the activity expressed "outward," towards the external world, represents extraversion; in the second case, the activity expressed "inward," towards defending the organism, represents introversion.

By framing his description of the extraversion-introversion polarity in this way, no doubt Jung felt that this polarity had strong empirical significance which could not be wisely avoided or denied. It's part of our "biology." For this reason, in *Psychological Types* he spends what may seem to be a disproportionate amount of time on this polarity to finally conclude that ". . . we must treat the introverted and extraverted types as categories over and above the function-types" (CW 6, para. 836). One does well to keep this emphasis in mind when independently comparing Jungian typology with various extensions or modifications of the theory that build on less firm hypotheses.

In his "position-papers" at the end of the book, Jung more explicitly develops his understanding of the two attitude-types by focusing on the constant modifications between subject and object (agent and scene, organism and environment). That is, "subject" and "object" increasingly become for Jung the operative terms upon which both extraversion and introversion are to be analyzed. Jung's concern with object-relations can be seen to connect with and be more fully developed in the work of Guntrip (1969), Fairbairn (1954), Winnicott (1965), and others.

In the most familiar, behavioral terms, the following broad sketches can act as reference points for making future observations about the attitude-types and their respective object-relations in everyday settings.[5]

To the extravert, the object is fascinating and valuable, making the relationship to the world typically open, sociable, and active. Because stimulation comes from the outside, this person may feel naturally pulled into the world, trying to stay busy by doing many things at once. The typical extravert has a consummate desire to influence others and/or the environment, but is as likely to be influenced by the surrounding conditions of his or her own life as well.

Theoretically, extraverts usually seem confident, accessible, and expansive (even "imperialistic") in the manner in which they move around in the world. They may also have a tendency to "think out loud," and are themselves usually very tolerant of noises or interruptions.

To introverts, extraverts may seem alternately congenial or intrusive, gregarious or obnoxious, encouraging or pushy, as the case may be. They may also appear as "busy-bodies" or "always wanting center-stage," and their action-oriented lifestyle can make an introvert cringe.

By contrast, the introvert relates to the object by turning in. To the introvert, the object is seen as draining energy away from the more important subjective world, and so this person acts to withdraw energy from the object to prevent it from gaining influence or control. The introvert's attitude is then an abstracting one. By withdrawing the energy from the object, the introvert effectively conserves it for his/her own position. All of this inclines introverts to be somewhat more independent and idea-oriented than extraverts, as they get their stimulation from the interior or subjective world.

Theoretically, introverts may seem lost in thought, or somewhat inaccessible or reserved in the way they move around the world. Unlike the extravert, the introvert may feel pushed by the world, and so place a high value on solitude and quiet. It is not unusual for an introvert to express this need for privacy by appearing somewhat "territorial," or protective of his or her "space."

To extraverts, introverts may seem alternately reflective or withdrawn, intense or detached, profound or weird, as the case may be. They may also appear as nonparticipatory in group activities, "stuck-up" or a "drag."

It needs to be emphasized in our discussion of extraversion and introversion that Jung believed each mode of orientation can work equally well, given that it is the natural or authentic orientation of an aware individual. However, because of the dominance, primacy, and respectability of the object in our own extraverted culture, we often view introverted behavior with great suspicion. Common judgments about a person's psychology, such as "What's wrong with him anyway? Why is he so shy? Why doesn't he fit in? Does he just hate people? What's she so paranoid about?" etc., actually tell more about the person talking than the person talked about (an extravert no doubt talking about an introvert). Even the relatively young discipline of psychology often defines the symptomatology of maladjustment, narcissistic/borderline and neurotic/psychotic states in terms that assume a kind of collective "extraversion" as the norm or criterion for diagnosis.

While introversion can indicate pathology, extraversion can as well, and with Jung's typology, as we will see, we are never given simple divisions which allow the labeling process to do all the work for us. Jung, a strong introvert himself, was always cautious about cutting off the odd, unusual, or "maladaptive" behaviors that did not seem to fit into conventional frames of reference. He often talked about the insights his patients had given him simply in exchange for his knowing how to listen to them. In this vein, he would warn prospective analysts:

> Personal and theoretical prejudices are the most serious obstacles in the way of psychological judgment . . . the patient is there to be treated and not to verify a theory. For that matter, there is no single theory in the whole field of practical psychology that cannot on occasion prove basically wrong. (CW 16, para 237)

If one reads enough of Jung, one can more than safely say that insofar as his typological categories are concerned, these sentiments apply to his own theoretical work as well. In any case, such thinking on Jung's part no doubt prompted Laurens van der Post to remark convincingly that Jung "was much closer to his patients than to his profession" (1975, p. 111). But because of Jung's "theoretical virtuosity," the casual reader may slight Jung's emphasis on the primacy of the patient in favor of his more elaborate, formal constructions.

Often it is this theoretical virtuosity that causes some people to react to Jung's type categories from what is probably best called a "purist mentality." They believe Jung is trying to say to them, for example, that all people are trapped in either an exclusively extraverted or an exclusively introverted orientation. A "pure" attitude-type in that sense would surely need help, as would the theorist who came up with the notion. Most people can readily recognize both introverted and extraverted behaviors as valued parts of their individual personalities.

However, Jungian typology draws on habitual or naturally preferred behaviors: "When any of these attitudes is habitual, thus setting a definite stamp on the character of an individual, I speak of a psychological type" (CW 6, para. 835). Being extraverted, then, does not prevent an individual from introverted behavior, nor vice versa, though one attitude is very often characteristic of a specific personality in the sense that that person seems best able to agree with it, i.e., the person is more comfortable and feels truer to him- or herself (ego-identified) in one attitude rather than another. This reasoning will similarly apply when we discuss the Jungian function-types.

This matter of "agreeing" or "harmonizing" with something taken as natural to and distinctive of the personality, and at the same time revealing underlying and universal patterns, is of preeminent significance to Jung in his "psychology of consciousness" (a telling alternative description which Jung himself used to designate his typology). Consciousness, for Jung, can be thought of as an individual's awareness of his or her own personality. Jungian typology, then, is a way of putting the individual into conscious and active participation with the broad lines in his or her own personality. Typological patterns are in turn often very characteristic of the ego of the individual, which for Jung is the central complex of consciousness itself.

A therapeutic point which Jung makes about attitude-type perhaps best demonstrates the significance of these categories and also provides a way to understand which attitude-type an individual may in fact be. In this example, the general issue centers around extraverts who are *prevented* from extraverting (or conversely, introverts from introverting), or introverts who are continually *forced* to extravert (conversely, extraverts forced to habitually introvert). Jung asserts that all of these individuals run the risks of future neuroses due to what he calls a "falsification of type" (CW 6, para. 560). We must interpret this as being in a state of disagreement or disharmony with oneself, or lacking consciousness of oneself, or from an ethical point of view, lying to oneself, or from a strictly psychological point of view, having a "false I."

"Falsification of type" could happen for a variety of reasons, many having to do with outside, coercive influences. One such influence to which Jung points has to do with parenting. It is through this example that Jung gives us a hint to help us identify our own attitude preference.

> As a rule, whenever falsification of type takes place as a result of parental influence, the individual becomes neurotic later, and can be cured only by developing the attitude consonant with his nature . . . a reversal of type often proves exceedingly harmful to the physiological well-being of the organism, usually causing acute exhaustion. (CW 6, paras. 560–561)

By observing which attitude tires us out the most and the quickest when we are using it, we may extrapolate from the above comments and make a fairly good guess at our own individual attitude-type. A safe bet is that the resultant fatigue is a sure giveaway of the attitude-type we are NOT. Moreover, constant fatigue or exhaustion may be indicative of a "falsification of type," which may reasonably point us to examining the parent/child relationship, all the while staying attentive to the individual's need to develop "the attitude consonant with one's nature."

By understanding extraversion and introversion in context of characteristic preferences and reflective of more or less natural and distinguishable differences among individuals, these terms become less offensive or imposing.

Before going any further with our discussion of attitude-types, we must now come to some understanding of the dynamics of Jungian typology. This takes us to the age-old concept of "polar opposites," a concept which was introduced earlier, when we set up the oppositions between extraversion-introversion, thinking-feeling, and sensation-intuition. A proper understanding of polarity and the specific use which Jung makes of it in his typology will provide a philosophical guard against the purist mentality mentioned earlier and give us significant insight into one of the meta-principles animating all of Jung's work as well. This emphasis will also help us to better appreciate the importance of the problem of opposites in Jung's psychology as a whole.

Polarity is probably best understood by meditating on a few fragments from the pre-Socratic philosopher Heraclitus of Ephesus, who lived about 500 B.C. We only have one book of fragments from Heraclitus, but these fragments cover all the metaphysical, scientific, and political knowledge of his time. Heraclitus himself is probably best known for perhaps three fragments out of the 139 in existence: "Character for man is destiny," "It is not possible to step into the same river twice," and "War is both king of all and father of all" (Freeman, 1957).

Though Jung was surely very familiar with the body of Heraclitian fragments which have come down to us, little direct documentation exists to warrant presenting Heraclitus's work as a bonafide Ur-text for Jung's notion of polarity as he develops it in his typology.[6] Only three references to Heraclitus in all of *Psychological Types* are cited in the index (though all significant ones).

However, Jung had such a strong integrative grasp of so many excellent sources, and his deference to Heraclitus is so obvious in his other books, that I do not feel hesitant about invoking a few fragments at this time to help demonstrate this critical issue in Jungian psychology. Although a look at almost any grouping of the Heraclitian fragments would do, the most helpful and pertinent ones for our purposes seem to be the following:

> #8. That which is in opposition is in concert and from things that differ comes the most beautiful harmony.
>
> #51. They do not understand how that which differs with itself is in agreement: harmony consists of opposing tension, like that of the bow and the lyre.
>
> #60. The way up and down are one and the same.
>
> #67. God is day-night, winter-summer, war-peace, satiety-famine. But he changes like fire which when it mixes with the smoke of incense, is named according to each man's pleasure.
>
> #88. What is in us is the same thing: living and dead, awake and sleeping, young and old: for each pair of opposites having changed becomes the former, and this again having changed becomes the latter.
>
> #125. The mixed drink also separates if it is not stirred.
>
> #126. Cold things grow hot, hot things grow cold, and the wet dries, the parched is moistened.

After the initial shock of contradiction and seeming irrationality, even these few fragments have enough force in them to strike us with the immediacy of thought itself and the playfulness of language in disrupting common perceptions to suggest alternative points of view.

Heraclitus is trying to have us experience what is probably best described as thoughts on the razor's edge. He is struggling with a vantage point or perspective that is strangely alert to its own intellectual conditions, and to how those conditions paradoxically subvert phenomena, even the phenomenon of trying to know or understand itself.

The philosophical complaint behind the fragments seems to be that we neglect the oppositional nature of all life and the characteristic movement of change and transformation which is fundamental to that opposition. We would rather content ourselves by dividing the opposites, forcing an unnatural stability between them, and so come to understand and identify one end of the pole at the expense of the other. Heraclitus seems to say that such "understanding" is an illusion. Instead, he would suggest that life is made up everywhere of pairs of opposites which are at once irreconcilable as well as inseparable. Moreover, the "poles" of the opposites are best perceived as moving through a natural process of transformation and change of one into the other. Heraclitus uses the word *enantiodromia* to focus on this phenomenon, a term which Jung will openly incorporate into his own psychology.

This concept of *enantiodromia* is absorbed into one of the premier organizing principles which Jung never abandoned in his overall psychology, what he termed "the law of compensation." Because of its central importance to Jungian psychology as a whole and its connection with the Heraclitian fragments, a lengthy passage from *Psychological Types* is now warranted. This particular passage is especially effective both for what is said and the clarity with which Jung says it.

> The activity of consciousness is selective. Selection demands direction. But direction requires the exclusion of everything irrelevant. This is bound to make the conscious orientation (q.v.) one-sided. The contents that are excluded and inhibited by the chosen direction sink into the unconscious, where they form a counterweight to the conscious orientation. The strengthening of this counter position keeps pace with the increase of conscious one-sidedness until finally a noticeable tension is produced . . . The more one-sided the conscious attitude, the more antagonistic are the contents arising from the unconscious, so that we may speak of a real opposition between the two . . . As a rule, the unconscious compensation does not run counter to consciousness, but is rather a balancing or supplementing of the conscious orientation . . . Normally, compensation is an unconscious process, i.e., an unconscious regulation of conscious activity. In neurosis the unconscious appears in such stark contrast to the conscious state that compensation is

disturbed. The aim of analytical therapy, therefore, is the realization of unconscious contents in order that compensation may be re-established. (C.W. 6, paras. 694–695)

This law of compensation was for Jung, as he stated, part of the self-regulatory nature of the psyche. When the law of compensation is "broken," then restoration or a return to "order," or perhaps better, balance or harmony, becomes a goal of analytical therapy itself.

Perhaps as important for our purposes, though, the law of compensation allows Jung to recognize opposing aspects of any phenomenon in a manner which gives the fragments of Heraclitus modern psychological meaning. This is to say that the extraversion-introversion *polarity* is the issue for Jung, not simply extraverting or introverting. For when one is consciously extraverting, something has happened to the other half of the polarity, something less detectable because it is no longer conscious, but just as real in terms of meaning for the whole individual.

For Jung, energy going out signifies extraversion at a conscious level *as well as* introversion at the unconscious level. What appears to define or characterize consciousness is "true," i.e. extraverts turn their energy away from their subjective selves toward the object. But what goes on at the unconscious level is equally "true": in this case, the unconscious would have a markedly introverted orientation which compensates, balances, and makes whole the appearance of its more obvious opposite operating in consciousness. For the neurotic, this compensation process is "disturbed," seeming to work against the conscious position, encroaching and "negatively" influencing the individual.

It is when the balance between conscious and unconscious life is seriously upset, when the law of compensation is violated, that we can imagine one pole in the psyche behaving as though the other pole did not exist. In these instances, one may expect a "fight," "conflict," or "disagreement" to create a new balance within the overall personality. The opposing sides of the individual's psyche will then often "tense up" and cause actual and distinguishable physical manifestations (symptoms) as the personality undergoes the process toward growth, transformation, or reconciliation with itself. You may hear the individual in the middle of the transformation process comment about being "out of character," or in more telling colloquialisms, being "beside himself," "strung-out," "bent out of shape," "put off," "really steamed," "out-of-joint," "ready to blow", "all torn up inside," "in pieces," "at the end of my rope," "stressed-out," "ready to break," "ready to explode," etc. These are all phrases which in very concrete language dramatically demonstrate the general disjointedness of ego-consciousness out of balance with the unconscious.

In *Psychological Types* there are many examples of the need to understand the psyche in terms of polarity and the law of compensation. One which is pertinent to the extraversion-introversion polarity and illustrative of the dynamics of Jungian typology as a whole has to do with what Jung calls "the harmful consequences of an exaggeration of the extraverted attitude" (CW 6, para. 569).

In light of our study so far, we should have a fuller understanding of what Jung is getting ready to point to here. Jung is saying that the apparently outward-directed extravert who overdoes his or her extraversion creates, in the unconscious, the missing part to the whole picture, namely the highly subjective introvert. Using the word coined by Heraclitus, an enantiodromia, or tendency of one thing to turn into its opposite, then makes itself present in the conscious life of the individual . . . in often unsettling, disagreeable, and even harmful ways.

In this example, the extravert's normally public and generous personality may seem to turn egotistical or excessively demanding. Or this person who otherwise may be known for being congenial and considerate of others could become arbitrarily forceful, ruthless, self-absorbed, aggressive, or otherwise inconsiderate. In both behavior patterns, the person is in effect acting unconsciously, through a suppressed and inferior introversion familiar neither to the conscious ego nor to others close to the person. Combine the often unseemly efforts of the unconscious to make itself recognized during the process of transformation and the individual pulling away from these efforts in such strenuous and determined (exaggerated) manners, and one realizes how easily problems are compounded and issues confused.

We need not focus only on the exaggerated extravert. Reversing the emphasis, we could envision what may be ahead for the exaggerated introvert. An introvert who accents or overplays his or her own introversion constellates in the unconscious the extravert who is in a sense overstimulated and overwhelmed with the world's significance. The object now has been magnified beyond belief at the unconscious level in compensation for its devaluation at the conscious level.

Should the unconscious have to force its way into consciousness, the exaggerated introvert may take on an artificially placating posture in which attempts are now made to be all things to all people. In this case, an excess of politeness, civility, and attachment is often used to mediate between a fearful subject and domineering objects. While this introvert may seem to be functioning well and in a mannerly way, the behaviors could as likely be hiding an individual who may actually be at the mercy of the object, "bowled over" by what the world seems to be offering or demanding, and at the same time lost to what seems to be the world's inscrutable and inexorable powers. In this sense, the introvert's behaviors may become erratic, explosive, excessively showy, or otherwise unpredictable. This same individual could equally find him- or herself so fearful of the outer world that every effort is made to overcome, control, or dominate that world.

The dynamic between conscious and unconscious life as brought into play through the specific and distinguishing behaviors of extraversion or introversion can obviously lead to a variety of behaviors, dangerous as well as subtle in design and structure. However, all the while it is worth noting that the etiology is the same. Because of this, the conflicts and eruptions in everyday interactions often seem hopelessly complicated and hard to identify, but still not entirely beyond our understanding. This is perhaps the not insignificant hope which Jung's typology ultimately holds out for us.

The problem on all fronts is that consciousness is never sufficiently or ordinarily aware of its rootedness in the unconscious, and so is always vulnerable to being manipulated by it in an infinite number of ways. In a sense, consciousness emerges from the unconscious in such a way that even at its best it will always have an "unfinished" edge about it. This edge is the ever-present boundary between consciousness and the unconscious, the blur between knowing and not-knowing. In this sense, the ongoing project of ego-consciousness is to be "educated," to make itself aware of its connection to the unconscious and the boundary condition which so defines it, not to outdistance or deny its roots. To pull oneself away from the unconscious in this manner is to invite suffering and a life lived at the mercy of the unconscious itself.

In reality, how one is "educated" to the effects of the unconscious always plays a telling and particular role in how a person works out his or her own individual personality and destiny. Typology itself is clearly a product of consciousness used to help to that end. In fact, it would not be too much to say that typology is the key to viewing consciousness itself as limited or expanded by its relationship to the unconscious. We are now very close to what Meier meant by his comment that "the individuation process begins and ends with typology."

Now, if not before, the person reading or learning about typology senses that his or her own unconscious must be taken into account just to be able to reliably use (i.e., consciously, maturely, responsibly, with any measure of sophistication or precision or honesty) the concepts which Jung himself is using. We begin to ask ourselves, "Are we behaving in a conscious manner, or is the unconscious expressing itself through us?"

This important question pertains not only to as strong and salient a distinction as extraversion and introversion, but to countless more subtle behaviors as well. That is, we theoretically come to the point where the insights being provided by Jung's formulations redound upon themselves and force one to take new account of one's own situation, point of view, and individuality. The typological category of extraversion-introversion has in effect served the prime and not insignificant purpose of provoking the individual to take him- or herself seriously *as a whole human being.*

One also becomes aware of an early "in-house" check to misusing typological observations, the implications of which go something like this: one's applications of typology to others can be no more effective or insightful than its application to one's own self-understanding. Jungian typology, for all its professed empirical reliability and objective analyses, ultimately takes one into the laboratory of one's own self. Or, in terms the new physics would appreciate, the observed cannot be understood apart from a taking account of the observer (Talbot, 1980).

To summarize: the movement of energy along the extraversion-introversion pole always implies a movement along the conscious-unconscious pole. Typology for Jung, then, is a psychology of consciousness which implies a psychology of the unconscious. With the concept of polarity and the law of compensation, Jungian typology has the dynamic principle it needs to distinguish and analyze movement back and forth between conscious and unconscious life, valuing both in constant and meaningful relationship.

In everyday life we would usually approach consciousness first, and later on attend to the unconscious as its presence forces itself on us. Jung makes it clear, however, that he is interested in a methodology for viewing both aspects of the personality at once. He starts with consciousness only because that is the "location" where the "problem" is first encountered and identified.

Finally, to recall Heraclitus: "the way up and the way down are one and the same." With Jung's typology, consciousness, traveling "up," is broadened or transformed by the opposite "truth," the unconscious, the way "down." The individuation process, the business of becoming who one is destined to be in relationship to the world and one's self, takes place when one is able to see "the way up" as where one is "now," but at any time in the journey, also recognizing and relating to the way down (the unconscious) as well.

The meta-principle of polarity thus helps to unhook us from too literal or fixed a reading of Jung's work and allows us to focus attention on the development of Jung's ideas. Mention is made of this now, because for many readers Jung's terminology for the "function-types" (sensation-intuition, thinking-feeling) may appear more idiosyncratic and so on less firm ground than the extraversion-introversion polarity.

The Functions

After Jung conceived of his typology based on the extraversion-introversion polarity, he went through a ten-year period of doubting these early formulations (CW 6, para. 944). Through his continued work on the "type-problem," he was forced to admit to himself that something was amiss. He comments,

> I had tried to explain too much in too simple a way . . . What struck me now was the undeniable fact that while people may be classed as introverts or extraverts, this does not account for the tremendous differences between individuals in either class. (Ibid.)

To achieve the subtlety and refinement which Jung felt appropriate to his observations on personality differences, he added the four basic functions, which he termed sensation, intuition, thinking, and feeling, and concluded that "strictly speaking, there are no introverts and extraverts pure and simple, but only introverted and extraverted function-types . . . " (CW 5, para. 913)

Jung confesses that he can give "no *a priori* reason for selecting these four functions as basic functions" (CW 6, para. 731), and relies fundamentally on his many years of clinical experience to make the distinctions. But, make no mistake about it, distinctions he intends them to be.

"Thinking," as Jung describes it, is absolutely different from "feeling"; "sensation" absolutely different from "intuition" (Ibid.). When a person is consciously engaged in one function, for that period of time it is separated out from the others, or as Jung terms it, the function is "differentiated." To the extent that a function is undifferentiated, it remains relatively unconscious and so of an ambivalent (mixed) and archaic nature (CW 6, para. 705). We should recall here the long passage on compensation, where Jung characterized consciousness as selective and directed. In fact, Jung considers differentiation "the essence, the *sine qua non* of consciousness" (CW 7, para. 339).

In Jung's observations, the selection and development of a particular function goes along in some way with the practical criteria of whatever works best for the particular individual. By this measure, this dominant or superior function can often be judged as a good, operative habit. Jung comments:

> Just as the lion strikes down his enemy or his prey with his fore-paw, in which his specific strength resides, and not with his tail like the crocodile, so our habitual mode of reaction is normally characterized by the use of our most reliable and efficient function, which is an expression of our particular strength. (CW 6, para. 947)

The superior function thus is characterized by strength, confidence, preference, comfort, and getting results. When any one function habitually dominates consciousness in this manner, a corresponding function-type results which may itself be either introverted or extraverted, depending on the subject's relationship to the object, as we discussed earlier.

With four functions and two attitudes, Jung's typology is suddenly able to formally generate eight personality types. One could speak for example of an "extraverted thinking-type," implying someone whose attention is habitually turned toward the object and away from the subject, with the thinking-function as characteristic of the preferred and conscious means of adaptation. Or, we could formulate a picture of an "introverted feeling-type," implying someone whose attention is habitually turned inward to the subject, with the feeling function as characteristic of the preferred and conscious means of adaptation. (The remaining six types would be designated extraverted sensing, extraverted intuiting, extraverted feeling, introverted sensing, introverted intuiting, introverted thinking.)

To understand the meanings of any of these possible combinations, however, we will need to further flesh out Jung's terminology, much as we did with the extraversion-introversion polarity. This exercise will help us with the actual observations of everyday behaviors according to function types.

First, notice needs to be taken of the words "rational" or "judging," which Jung uses interchangeably to describe the polarity of thinking-feeling. By referring to thinking-feeling as the rational or judging function-types, Jung is intending to call attention to general similarities within the glaring differences

of the pair of opposites at hand. Thinking and feeling are similar because they both operate according to discriminating and
evaluative principles. However, one function's evaluative
principles are most easily associated with the head, and the
other function's evaluative principles are most often connected with the heart; one with ordering and judging to reach an
objective and logical conclusion, the other with attaching a
proper and personal value. Most importantly for Jung, one
cannot consciously think and feel at precisely the same time.
Using one function habitually pushes the other into the
unconscious, for not-so-safe keeping, as we have seen.

Let us look at each "rational" or "judging" function in the
superior or dominant position. "Feeling" used in Jung's sense
is perhaps the most troublesome of the four terms he uses to
distinguish the four functions. He means to view feeling as
"a kind of judgment, different from intellectual judgment in
that its aim is not to establish conceptual relations but to set
up a subjective criterion of acceptance or rejection" (CW 6,
para. 724).

The common perception that feeling-types are high-
strung or emotional is against Jung's intentions in using this
designation. Any type is capable of strong emotion. Jung here
is instead drawing attention to a difference in criteria for
forming judgments which could best be described as a preference for the personal over the impersonal. To highlight the
complexity of this function, Jung wryly comments, "The
very notion of classification is intellectual and therefore
incompatible with the nature of feeling" (CW 6, para. 728).

Because of the emphasis on the personal and subjective,
feeling-types often value harmony and human relationships.
They are relatively accepting or trusting and both need and
extend appreciation. Feeling-types may tend to be effusive or
sentimental, but are also especially capable of attachment or
sympathy. They generally have an aptitude or talent for
knowing what matters most to themselves and to other people and can be very adept at handling interpersonal situations
or problems.

In the vernacular, "feeling" is probably best understood as
it is expressed in such phrases as "I do (or do not) like that,"
i.e., a subjective value is established based on likes and dis-
likes. When one hears such comments as "I'm uncomfortable

with that," "That didn't please me," "Can't you be more understanding," "Try giving that person the benefit of the doubt," "I have something to share with you," one is probably safe in assuming that the feeling function has been brought into play. After talking with a feeling-type, one may "feel" how utterly complicated and impossible human relationships are. To a feeling-type, on the other hand, this complexity and involvement would make relationships all the more valuable. One needs to keep in mind that the feeling function, like all four functions, means something qualitatively different in regard to whether it is working through extraversion or introversion.

The opposite function to "feeling" Jung designates "thinking," the other rational or judging function. As Jung expresses it, "Thinking, following its own laws, brings the contents of ideation into conceptual connection with one another" (CW 6, para. 830). In contrast to feeling, thinking emphasizes logic and objectivity in reasoning through to correct and truthful conclusions. As such, thinking suppresses or subordinates personal values or attachments.

Thinking-types are capable of abstracting principles to make distinctions and definitions which apply to the otherwise chaotic or confusing mass of material bombarding the individual. They can also use those principles to cut into, analyze, or criticize the matter at hand. Thinking-types tend to be impersonal or firm minded, and can be argumentative, critical, or blunt in their human relationships. Because they calculate for consequences, they are often thought of as manipulative of situations in ways that suggest an interest in power or intimidation. This, of course, is not always the case.

The thinking function can produce such injunctions as "Be logical," "Be objective," "Don't let your heart rule your head," "Be clear about what you're saying," "Let's find out exactly what's at stake," "Define your terms," "Do you really know what you are getting into?" One may even be convinced after talking to a thinking-type that whatever one has had to suffer by way of criticism, correction, or "enlightenment," at least one may have been brought a little closer to the truth.

Thinking and feeling as rational or judging functions are contrasted with the "irrational" or "perceiving" functions, which Jung equates with the polarity of sensation-intuition. By designating sensation and intuition as irrational or perceiving functions, Jung wants to call attention to the flow of what is happening without regard to how it is organized, evaluated, ordered, or judged.

Sensation and intuition are similar because they both operate in a nondiscriminatory or noninterfering manner with the material at hand. They are irreconcilably different because they are predisposed to take in qualitatively different kinds of information. Sensation is perception via conscious sensory activity, and so is opposed to intuition, which Jung understands to be conscious perception via the unconscious (CW 6, para. 951). In some sense, intuition is a special function to Jung and will be dealt with last. For now, once again, it is important to realize that one cannot consciously be using both sensation and intuition precisely at the same time. To use either function habitually pushes the other function into the unconscious.

"Sensation," Jung defines, "is the psychological function that mediates the perception of a physical stimulus" (CW 6, para. 461). On the surface this term is the easiest to understand and apply. Jung is referring to the preference an individual may have for direct experience through the senses. Sensation is designated as an irrational or perceiving function because Jung believes it has to do with elementary "facts," or taking in things as they are without tracing them back to reason or rational formulations. Jung concludes, "Since sensation is an elementary phenomenon, it is given a priori, and unlike thinking and feeling, is not subject to rational laws" (CW 6, para. 796).

Because sensing-types are so interested in reality as it is presented to them, they tend to be factual and very observant, and they are capable not only of "seeing" but of remembering those facts and details. They may have a tendency to be conservative or reluctant to change in the sense that what is present, apparent, and obvious is more than enough world for them. They also seem to have more than their share of "common sense," often approaching a problem in a carefully deliberate, step by step way which shows a simple and accurate grasp of the immediate and practical aspects of the issue at hand.

In the vernacular, one may hear the sensing function in action when someone is asking one to "Be specific," "Be realistic," "Be practical," "Get your facts straight," or "Get back down to earth." You even may be reassured when a sensing-type tells you that "everything will get back to normal sooner or later."

"Intuition" is the counterpole to sensation, and is defined by Jung as "that function that mediates perceptions in an unconscious way . . . a kind of instinctive apprehension, no matter of what contents" (CW 6, para. 770). Because Jung directly connects intuition with the unconscious, this function reads in his work as somewhat privileged among the four, though only insofar as it provides a special link to that world which so fascinated Jung and which he felt was so unavoidable. In a sense, intuition becomes a preferred receptivity to the unconscious—something very handy to have around if your work routinely takes you to the unconscious. Otherwise, intuition can be understood in the same manner as the other functions, in definition against its polar opposite.

If the sensing function is tied to the earth, the intuitive function flies high in the sky. In fact, intuition needs to look at things from afar or vaguely in order to get a sense of the whole over the parts. It is from that vantage point too that intuition plays into imagination, speculation, and dreams of the possible. By not being "distracted" by details in the everyday world, intuition runs free and mixes in with everything that is hidden, invisible, or behind the scenes and senses. Accordingly, intuitive-types see "connections" everywhere. Because intuition is privileged to this other kind of information, it often can help one to see things from different, unusual, or alternative perspectives as well.

Intuitive-types also seem to be quick to take things in. They have an attraction for complexity, almost for its own sake. They appreciate the odd world of symbols and myth and often feel more at home in that world than what their immediate environment may offer. They can see abstract, theoretical, even universal relationships that convey meanings above and beyond the obvious. And as a general rule, they are not as apprehensive of change or novelty as their sensing-type counterparts may tend to be.

In the vernacular, intuition is probably best understood as that "sixth sense," that ability to "know" something in an unconventional manner often before anyone else or before something definite happens to make it clear to others. When someone "feels it in the air," whatever "it" is, intuition is probably at work. Or when someone is excited about a complex or interesting pattern that otherwise seems nonsensical or incoherent, that person's intuition is probably making meaningful connections. Listening to an intuitive-type will take one through endless suggestions, speculations, and possibilities, maybe even inspiring one to "take wings," "dream," or "imagine" for oneself.

These brief descriptions of the four functions are meant to be suggestive of the contrasts Jung is trying to highlight. As in the extraversion-introversion polarity, broad strokes were used to establish familiar points of reference. After we have marked out our contrasts among the four functions, another facet of Jung's typological theory arises for consideration.

The four functions taken together form a very powerful picture of the whole of reality. "Sensation establishes what is actually present, thinking enables us to recognize its meaning, feeling tells us its value, and intuition points to possibilities as to whence it came and whither it is going in a given situation," as Jung concisely puts it (CW 6, para. 958). Because each function plays its part in connecting us with the whole of reality, Jung refers to the four functions together as a "totality."

The four points on a compass would be a suitable metaphor for what Jung is trying to describe by referring to the notion of "totality." In fact, at one point in *Psychological Types*, Jung takes on the wayward navigator's persona and refers to himself as Columbus, typology as his compass, and the resulting psychological insights parallel to the discovery of America (CW 6, para. 936).

However one may feel about this particular composite metaphor, the four functions as Jung separates and then recombines them in his theory do give a particular feeling of completeness and stability of form. Indeed, when one begins to think about it, the number four has a connotative value of wholeness and stability that historically and culturally seems to transcend time and place, as Jung tirelessly pointed out. One thinks of the four seasons, 4/4 time in music, the four movements of a symphony, the four corners of the earth, the four elements (earth, water, fire, air), the four gospels, the four humors or temperaments (phlegmatic, sanguine, choleric, melancholic), the four forces in the universe (strong, weak, gravitational, electromagnetic), etc. All parts of the "four" are absolutely separate and different, and yet they combine to establish a unique, interesting, and meaningful whole. Jung's typology does not, of course, automatically carry this attribute of wholeness or completeness; that would be left for the individual to experience. But, metaphorically at least, one can begin to see how Jung's theoretical formulations can suggest the richness and variety one expects to encounter in the whole of reality.

In the final three pages of his general description of the eight possible personality types, Jung adds yet another refinement to his typology by introducing what he terms the auxiliary function. So far we have examined the attitude-types of extraversion-introversion and the four function-types: thinking, feeling, sensation, and intuition. The dynamics of typology are such that for any individual any function can act as the superior function in consciousness in either the extraverted or introverted attitude. The remaining attitude and functions, however, coexist in the unconscious in a compensatory manner to the superior attitude and function. We have seen too that when consciousness goes too far in one direction, whatever is suppressed in the unconscious becomes activated and may come unpredictably into play through the other functions and opposite attitude. This can have the effect of subverting or sabotaging the conscious orientation and functioning of the "normal," day-to-day personality. Jung comments: "Closer investigation shows with great regularity that besides the most differentiated function, another, less differentiated function of secondary importance is invariably present in consciousness and exerts a co-determining influence" (CW 6, para. 666). Furthermore, he tells us, this function of "secondary importance" is not a random one out of the remaining three, but one that is "different in every respect from the nature of the primary function" (CW 6, para. 667).

Jung's stipulation amounts to another symmetry being asserted in his theory. For if this secondary function must be "different in every respect," thinking theoretically cannot team up with feeling in consciousness because they are both rational or judging functions. Likewise, sensation cannot team up with intuition in consciousness because they are both irrational or perceiving functions. Theoretically speaking, thinking must team up with either sensation or intuition, as must feeling; and, sensation must team up with thinking or feeling, as must intuition.

By positing the auxiliary function in this manner, Jung has effectively asserted that consciousness normally acts from a balanced position of its own, drawing in information from one perceiving or irrational function and ordering that information through one of the judging or rational functions. That is, when a perceiving function is superior, a judging function serves as auxiliary in a codeterminant role; when a judging function is superior, a perceiving function serves as auxiliary in a codeterminant role.

When one takes into consideration the heightened and specific role of the auxiliary function, the number of conscious personality types in which one could generate formal psychological descriptions has now increased to sixteen, with an equal number of "counter-personalities" for the unconscious.[7]

As one example, it is now possible to talk about an "extraverted thinking-type with sensing," meaning an extravert with thinking as a superior function and sensing as an auxiliary function. All terms would be acting as modifying agents for the conscious personality, and compensated at the unconscious level by a "counter-personality" called an "introverted feeling-type with intuition." Something now must be briefly mentioned about these "counter-personalities" which start to become imposing figures on their own in the theory.

Just as each of the sixteen conscious personalities can be viewed as arranged around one of the four functions in combination with an auxiliary function and attitude, sixteen counter-personalities can be identified in the unconscious, each arranged around the opposite of the superior function, the function furthest removed from consciousness. Jung calls this most troublesome fourth function "the inferior function." We can infer that any of the sixteen "counter-personalities" which build up around any of the four functions in this "inferior" position would tell us about what has been suppressed and what the individual is particularly vulnerable to. One can immediately see, too, how the inferior function becomes a challenging and interesting topic on its own in analytical psychology (von Franz, 1984). For this reason, special treatment in a separate chapter will be necessary to better come to terms with this concept.

This is perhaps all the better. Some readers no doubt are ready to scream out loud at what has evolved from six apparently simply and familiar terms to a quagmire of nuance and complexity. Others may be starting to detect conceptual problems even if the symmetry in the theory remains appealing. As we have done the former group the favor of putting off a discussion of the "inferior function," let us address a conceptual problem in behalf of the "superior thinkers" in the latter group.

If the auxiliary function is in consciousness, as Jung stipulates, then the auxiliary would have to be in the same attitude as the superior function (either extraversion or introversion). This is due to the law of compensation: an attitude in consciousness is compensated by the opposing attitude in the unconscious. However, this would be a logical contradiction to Jung's remark that the auxiliary is "different in every way" from the superior or dominant function.

A theoretical question now arises: does, for example, an "extraverted thinker with sensing" consciously extravert his sensing, or is sensing introverted and so unconscious? If the former, Jung's description of the auxiliary as "different in every way" needs revision, for the auxiliary is in the same attitude as the superior; if the latter, then the auxiliary must be understood as different in its attitude by virtue of being unconscious, and again Jung's description of the auxiliary as functioning in consciousness needs revision.

In his work, we see Jung take both positions at different times. At one point Jung suggests that the superior function is so strong in consciousness that it is compensated in the unconscious by all three of the remaining functions in the opposite attitude. This reasoning would make the auxiliary function different in every way, but unconscious. At another time, he emphasizes the role of the auxiliary function in consciousness and so puts it in the same attitude as the superior function, either introverted or extraverted as the case may be.

This theoretical issue is still unresolved among many of Jung's successors. My personal opinion will be reviewed in more detail in Chapter VI, which is on type development and the individuation process. I feel Jung gives us better hints of what he was trying to get at in *Analytical Psychology, the Seminar Given in 1925,* than in *Psychological Types,* which I will make use of later. For the time being, however, I believe the auxiliary function is most often in the opposite attitude of the superior function and is *relatively* unconscious, i.e., it is more easily at the service of consciousness and the superior function than the remaining two functions. I do not think Jung's confusion on this issue as he struggles with it in *Psychological Types* need deter us any further for now.

Perhaps now we have reached the point where a test should be arranged to illustrate what we know of the theory. In the next chapter, we will use typology to critique typology. First, we will posit Jung's personality type. Then we will generate from the theory a proper devil's advocate, Jung's typological opposite, or counter-personality. This "Jungian critic" will get his day in court to critique Jung's own work.

The premise of this exercise is a simple one: if we could use Jungian typology to elicit from this devil's advocate some distinguishing yet legitimate and critical questions which expose the theory in a new light, then Jung's purpose "to provide a critical psychology" (CW 6, para. 959) would seem to be well served.

Interestingly enough, it is the actual act of confrontation between these competing but credible points of view that becomes important in this exercise, not necessarily who wins the argument or debate. As such, the importance of listening over talking, or the significance of learning from the opposition over "taking sides" would be the established value if the exercise proves successful.

Notes

1. After completing this chapter, I found C. A. Meier's provocative statement as part of a presentation he made to the Fourth International Congress for Analytical Psychology. Entitled "Psychological Types and Individuation: A Plea for a More Scientific Approach in Jungian Psychology," Meier's paper as well as the rest of the pro-

ceedings from the Congress have been edited by Joseph Wheel-wright under the title *The Analytic Process: Aims, Analysis, and Training*, published in 1971 by Putnam (New York).

In the many years since Meier's speech, the widespread success and status of the MBTI would seem to indicate Meier's wish has been fulfilled. While I appreciate the scientific work being done with Jungian typology through more forceful use of the MBTI, I think it is now time to come to a better understanding of the "art-fulness" necessary to make Jungian typology a practical and sym-pathetic tool of self-exploration.

2. If honorary degrees are any indication of respectability or scholarship, Jung's should probably be mentioned. He received hon-orary doctorates from the universities of Calcutta, Benares, Alla-habad; from Clark University, Fordham University, Harvard Uni-versity, Oxford University, the University of Geneva, and the Federal Institute of Technology in Zürich. He was also an honorary fellow of the Royal Society of Medicine, London.

3. The "new physics" usually refers to quantum mechanics, which began with Max Planck's theory of quanta in 1900, and rela-tivity, which began with Albert Einstein's special theory of relativ-ity in 1905. Some references under Capra, F. and Zukav, G. in the bibliograhy.

4. See Jung's 1928 essay "Psychic Energy," in CW 8 (pp. 3–66). Also, Harding, E. (1963), *Psychic Energy.*

5. Any treatment of Jung's typological works has a section which describes the "types." But, some authors have devoted con-siderable effort and interest in extending the type descriptions. See especially the following:

Briggs-Myers, I. (1980). *Introduction to Type.* Palo Alto, CA: Consulting Psychologists Press.

Keirsey, D. and Bates, M. (1978). *Please Understand Me.* Del Mar, CA: Promethean Books.

Kroeger, O. and Thuesen, J. (1988). *Type Talk, or How to Determine Your Personality Type and Change Your Life.* New York: Delacorte Press.

Quenk, N. (1993). *Beside Ourselves.* Palo Alto, CA: Con-sulting Psychologists Press.

Singer, J. and Loomis, M. (1984). *Interpretive Guide for the Singer-Loomis Inventory of Personality.* Palo Alto, CA: Consulting Psychologists Press.

The custom of "characterizing" Jung's typological formulations is now at the point of a minor literary convention. For better or worse, these sketches and the ones provided later in our study are given somewhat in that vein.

6. A more direct and obvious source for the notion of "polarity," at least as Jung later encountered it, is the Chinese book of oracles called the *I Ching.* See especially the following:

> Wilhelm, R. (trans.) (1950, 1977). *The I Ching or Book of Changes,* English translation by C. F. Baynes; Foreword by C. G. Jung. (Bollingen series: XIX). Princeton: Princeton Univeristy Press.
> Wilhelm, H. (1960). *Eight Lectures on the I Ching.* (Bollingen series: LXII). Princeton: Princeton University Press.

7. For purposes of itemizing the sixteen types, I have listed them in a manner which pairs the "counter-personality" of one to the other.

extraverted thinking-type with sensing
introverted feeling-type with intuition

extraverted thinking-type with intuition
introverted feeling-type with sensing

extraverted feeling-type with sensing
introverted thinking-type with intuition

extraverted feeling-type with intuition
introverted thinking-type with sensing

extraverted sensing-type with thinking
introverted intuiting-type with feeling

extraverted sensing-type with feeling
introverted intuiting-type with thinking

extraverted intuiting-type with thinking
introverted sensing-type with feeling

extraverted intuiting-type with feeling
introverted sensing-type with thinking

III

Applications of Jungian Typology:
A Hermeneutics of Listening

It is a fact, which is constantly and overwhelmingly apparent in my practical work, that people are virtually incapable of understanding and accepting any point of view other than their own.

(CW 6, para. 847)

OUR GOAL in this section of our study is to use Jungian typology in order to provide us with an understanding of Jung's own psychological type. We will then put Jung up against his psychological counter-personality to see how he fares against some "typological" criticisms of his own theory. We will thereby learn a little more about Jung and his psychological type, demonstrate the effectiveness of typological theory, and highlight some self-critical aspects and limitations inherent in Jung's typological work.

However, we must begin this section with a disclaimer that has the effect of taking us somewhat off the direct path to meeting this goal. Since Jung is not here to authenticate or dispute what we will say about his psychological type (he believed himself to be introverted thinking with strong intuition), we must realize that our typological conclusions about him will be necessarily tentative. The fact of Jung's death presents us with a general question: how involved must one be with the individual undergoing typological analysis to feel confident about the particular application?

Although the formal aspects of Jung's theory readily make for varied applications, some applications would no doubt yield better results than others. It seems to me that certain criteria must therefore be proposed to distinguish applications based on optimal conditions for typological use from those applications based on less favorable conditions. In this regard, whether the "subject" is alive to interact with the user of typology seems more than a rhetorical consideration.

In addition, whenever we say anything about anyone using Jungian typology, what we say is always up for discussion. This fact points us to another critical question: how receptive is the user of typology to new considerations that affect the initial individual analysis and/or allow for modifications of Jung's original theory? The capacity to modify typological conclusions or renovate the theory itself is vital to ensuring the descriptive and explanatory power of Jung's original insights.

In applying typology to Jung, as in all historical applications, the temptation to "lock in" to typological determinations and so content oneself with one's findings is especially great. When one is restricted either to second-hand or historical evidence in applying typology, one is perhaps more inhibited about making changes to the initial individual analysis or to the theory itself. When the practitioner of typology is spared the personal confrontation with the individual for whom the application is intended, typological conclusions may sound strangely insulated from "real life," and the typological theory itself little more than an interesting parlor game.

It is my belief that the most accurate and meaningful typological observations depend on the willing interaction of the observer and the observed. Furthermore, this interaction presumes the respect of the user of typology for the "typed." Ideally then, though not necessarily, the "observed" is the actual and alive person engaged in dialogue with the observer. Another way of saying this is that there are indeed ways to "type" a dead man, a character in a novel, a celebrity, an author, a famous historical person, etc., but one would undertake such a task realizing obvious and inevitable limitations;

typological insights become more and more provisional the further one gets from the lived reality. Because of this belief in the importance of the immediate and direct encounter between the observer and the observed, we have some early business with which to deal before getting to Jung's own psychological type as determined through the historical sources.

Specifically, I feel it important first to make some general comments on how typology can be used in less distant or historically removed circumstances. In this regard, perhaps the most immediate and intimate environment for typological observations and revelations is the clinical setting between therapist and client, to which we now turn.

Applying typology in clinical settings involves the therapist in a certain spontaneous and imaginative activity that is difficult to explain and impossible to describe. Nonetheless, this activity is essential, as is the use of whatever technical expertise one has acquired concerning the theory itself. In brief, one must be able to use typological terminology and principles to detect patterns of behavior and response, and then image forth an integrated picture of what the client actually intends to communicate about his or her own individual psychology. This is a task that is as much art as it is science, and so it assumes the risks connected with either overplaying one's imagination and spontaneity, or overemphasizing one's technical expertise (principles, laws, terminology, etc.) associated with the theory. Either extreme will cause the theory to break down in actual application.

By overplaying the spontaneous and imaginative element in applications, the therapist in effect cuts the theory off from both himself and the client. This creates an unbridgeable gap between the theory and the everyday reality which the theory purports to explain and describe. In a sense, the theory flies off from the therapist and goes to live a life of its own, often taking therapist and client with it. Here the problem for the therapist lies in reconstructing a psychological type specific and familiar enough to place the particular client confidently and realistically ahead of all the other possible personalities which the theory helps determine. If the therapist becomes too self-indulgent with his or her imagination, at one time or another an individual client will seem-

ingly become for the therapist *all* of the sixteen types. In
effect, the therapist who allows this to happen countertrans-
fers his or her own experiences with the imaginative elements of typological theory to the client's situation. This in
turn causes the client to become for the therapist simply an
occasion to play with or explore the theory in a dilettantish
and eccentric fashion.

We may suspect in actuality that only an incurable psychotic or a wise man could be determined to be all sixteen
psychological types. Rather, the therapist using typology
must help the client identify his or her own psychological
type in a manner that is specific enough to reflect the client's
particular ego-pattern as well as broad enough to connect
him with the common lot of humanity.

By overelaborating the technical aspects of the theory, the
therapist can come to equally bad results: the therapist uses
typological laws, principles, and terminology to create too
tight a structure to allow the client to function or act in a
self-authenticating manner. For the person who could otherwise make good use of typological insights, such misuse of
typology by the therapist would convey a "boxed-in" feeling
that is easily picked up on and often found annoying by a
client. Contrarily, in special cases where individuals may be
earnestly or desperately looking for "boxes" to live in, we
may find any suggestion of structure (i.e., any of the possible
sixteen personality types with their attendant "dark-side"
counterparts) too easily and favorably adopted by certain
clients. This happens regardless of how appropriate or "true"
the particular application may be for the person.

In both of the above instances, the therapist's technique
has actually concealed rather than revealed the client's true
personality type. Both yield flawed diagnostic results and are
essentially fraudulent approaches to the therapeutic
encounter. If the client is to do his or her part in confirming
and making meaningful the particular psychological type
that is in fact appropriate to him or her, free and characteristic movement of the personality is an essential prerequisite.

With the proper blend of technique and imagination,
typological insights into individual personalities can be presented in a manner that seems almost second nature for the
therapist, and is often readily confirmed by the client. The

ultimate task for the therapist who is applying Jungian typology is then to be ready to receive often conflicting information from the client on behalf of the client's own best interests, evaluate that information in a typological context, and imaginatively present it back to the client in a language that reflects a realistic understanding of that particular client's personality as a whole—all of this to be done in one apparent flowing motion, no less. When this is done successfully, not only do the therapist's insights seem to have earned the client's assent and favor, but the client now has a credible starting point to begin to responsibly explore problems relating to his or her own particular psychology.

From a therapist's perspective, typology can also help to determine clinical approaches or treatment practices. An understanding of the client's emerging psychological type can facilitate the therapist's tailoring of treatment to the individual's own inclination towards a particular therapeutic modality. Especially interesting in this regard is the opening up of otherwise competitive psychological models and techniques which can now be entertained by the therapist as potentially useful with a client of a particular psychological type. For therapists who would otherwise "define" their allegiance with one approach or model only, typology can provide "permission" to be more creative in the therapeutic encounter. Because of this strange propensity of typological theory to suggest such connections between individuals and psychological models, Alex Quenk has gone so far as to remark that "typology provides the most appropriate and theoretically sound rationale for eclecticism in the conduct of psychotherapy" (1984, p. 35).

When Jungian typology works as we have so far discussed it, I think of it as setting into motion what I have termed a "hermeneutics of listening." By using this phrase I hope to describe a feature of sound clinical practice as well as to broaden the range of typology so that it may be successfully used by the layperson in everyday settings.

David Linge informs us that "hermeneutics has its origin in breaches in intersubjectivity" (Gadamer, 1976, p. xii). I take this to mean that when points of view are up for grabs, distorted or confused, obscured or buried, broken off or ill-communicated, hermeneutics comes into play. Linge goes on to describe the hermeneutical field as including "all those situations in which we encounter meanings that are not immediately understandable but require interpretive effort . . ." (Ibid.). The assumption here is that there is indeed a meaning available to be interpreted, or, for our purposes, a personality to be discovered or understood.

These "situations" which Linge talks about seem to me to be the points of departure which Jung calls attention to in the epigraph to this section of our study. In fact, I believe the "hermeneutical problem" as we have defined it is the main problem Jung addressed with his typology. Jung was after all interested in providing principles to guide us through certain breaches and ambiguities in human interaction, which by being properly interpreted become meaningful forms of communication between and among fellow human beings.

Another traditional use of the word "hermeneutics" recommends itself now for our purposes. As most of us are aware, the earliest situations in which principles of interpretation were formally worked out involved those religious texts whose meanings had been obscured by time or whose significance could not be brought into line with current cultural or political conditions. I do not think it inappropriate to address the human personality in as reverent a manner. The efforts behind typology can then be characterized as a conceptual elaboration of the forgotten or obscured "sacred truths" within the individual in his or her particular circumstances. The corollary to this assumption entails viewing the human personality as a "sacred text," and therefore innately worthy of careful attention and interpretation.

Finally, the emphasis on "listening" in our title is meant first to focus attention on the immediate and receptive mode which typology at its best asks from its user, and then to emphasize the everyday world of talk and conversation as a natural locus for typological investigations. Linge comments that "alienation from meaning can just as well occur while engaging in direct conversation" (Ibid.). I would assert that conversation properly interpreted, in or out of the clinical setting, is actually the best place to see the "type problem" in action . . . and the best place to "solve" type problems as well.

An implicit criticism of Jung's _Psychological Types_ may

now need to be made explicit. In the preface to the first Swiss edition, Jung tells us that his book was

> the fruit of nearly twenty years' work in the domain of practical psychology. It grew gradually in my thoughts, taking shape from the countless impressions and experiences of a psychiatrist in the treatment of nervous illnesses, from intercourse with men and women of all social levels, from my personal dealings with friend and foe alike, and finally, from a critique of my own psychological peculiarity. (CW 6, p. xi)

However, in Jung's actual text his determination to substantiate his theory in the history of ideas seemed to demand his best efforts, often masking the original inspiration of his work as he stated it above. Without taking anything away from Jung's vigorous and successful *tour de force* in the history of ideas, we now unabashedly return Jung's theory to the trenches of human interaction where it belongs, and so move future typological efforts to the dimension of actual and everyday human reality. Viewing typology as a "hermeneutics of listening," with all the immediacy and presence which the act of listening implies, is our way of shifting the emphasis forward—and back to Jung's original inspiration. At times in his book, Jung took this emphasis. And, no doubt his intentions lay in this direction as well. For the most part, however, he seemed less able or concerned to articulate this emphasis than to prove the theory's overall truth-value.

After all of the above is said, I nonetheless want to reemphasize that typology by definition deals with "typical" or representative behaviors and characteristics. In that sense, the true test of any psychological typology is to call proper attention from the best evidence at hand to those broad lines that differentiate the conscious and functioning personality. We are, after all, looking at what is relatively constant, habitual, and preferred about the individual, and should not be unduly modest or apologetic about our findings once we understand the theory and its limitations. This is Jung's own point of view in his lengthy cultural-historical analysis in the first three-fifths of his book. It is also the point of view we will now use to sanction our own typological observations about Jung himself.

Jung's Type

From what Jung has written, it is my opinion that he
extraverts his thinking function.[1] That is, his energy goes out
to the world in a way that implies logic and consequence, a
yearning for structure and objectivity, a critical, even self-
critical mode of analyzing situations, and a preference for
establishing and defining principles which can cut into and
guide him through his subject matter. Thinking is how he
primarily relates to the exterior world. But obviously this is
not the whole story.

Jung is by no means an extravert. His preference is clearly for the subjective world of ideas, reflection, solitude, and
interior stimulation. Since introversion is his dominant attitude, thinking must be serving—in the extraverted attitude—
as his auxiliary function, helping the as yet unspecified superior function which lives confidently, if somewhat hiddenly,
in the introverted orientation.

In keeping with our interpretation of the auxiliary function (see p. 49), we postulate that Jung's auxiliary function is
in the opposite attitude of his dominant function, and relatively unconscious. That is, the unconscious has enough of
an effect on Jung's extraverted thinking function to pose challenging, stimulating, and yet relatively "solvable" problems
for consciousness. His auxiliary function can therefore effectively move into consciousness in a characteristic manner
when necessity dictates.

We may also suspect that introverts such as Jung are
given added motivation to make more conscious use of their
auxiliary functions. They can appear to have a stronger preference for their auxiliary function than for their superior
function. This is simply because the exterior world of extraversion does not leave anyone out of its grasp, regardless of an
individual's preference. While it is difficult to imagine an
introvert spared the exigencies of the exterior world, it is not
so difficult to imagine an extravert living his or her life mer-
rily away with little or no attention to the interior world.
Almost by necessity, an introvert's auxiliary function will be
better developed than an extravert's auxiliary function.

To continue with our typological analysis: the truly char-

acteristic typological feature in Jung's personality, his dominant or superior function, seems beyond question. However,
because Jung is an introvert, one must look a little harder to
detect it. Any of Jung's biographies will give one a clear sense
of the supreme importance of intuition for Jung. Though
some biographers will quarrel with this function as too
"mystical," and others will be mesmerized by the insights it
is linked to, none of them fail to contend with it in detailing
both Jung's personal and professional life.

Intuition here refers to Jung's broad and imaginative reach
over so much material, his perception of the whole before the
parts, and his unmistakable attraction to and fascination
with the unconscious (which for Jung took projected form in
mythology, anthropology, poetry, art, and cross-cultural studies). Finally, it implies Jung's ability to make uncommon and
meaningful connections among otherwise odd or inaccessible
subjects.

In typological terms, then, we would make a provisional
but educated guess that Jung is an introvert with intuition
acting as his superior function and extraverted thinking serving as his auxiliary function. His opposite type, or what we
have been calling the "counter-personality," would be an
extravert with sensing as his superior function and introverted feeling as his auxiliary function.

At this point, the terminology, while cumbersome, is
extremely suggestive and could be used to spontaneously and
imaginatively generate two lengthy and competing points of
view toward any topic. We will, however, restrict ourselves
specifically to a few criticisms of Jung's typological theory
which can be suggested from the alternate point of view to
Jung's own psychological type.

Because Jung is not here to dialogue on the matter, I have
chosen to demonstrate this application of typology through an
imagined dialogue between Jung and his inner "adversary,"
whom we will call "Jabbok." This approach most definitely
runs the risk of that excess of imagination mentioned earlier.
We will nonetheless apply our "hermeneutics of listening" in
hopes that our "conversation" with Jung will not be too far off
the mark. Remember, an introverted intuitive-type with
extraverted thinking as his auxiliary function (Jung) is talking

with an extraverted sensing-type with introverted feeling as his auxiliary function (Jabbok). Let us see how this plays out.

Jabbok: I have tried and tried to read your *Psychological Types*. Some people whom I trust told me that I would find it useful in my everyday life.

C. G. Jung: Did you?

J: Did I read it, or did I find it useful?

CG: Both or either.

J: Well, actually I sort of half read it and found it . . . difficult.

CG: It sounds like you are hedging a bit. Please do not be so polite. I am interested in your honest reaction.

J: Well, I stopped at your discussion of Carl Spitteler's "Prometheus and Epimetheus." I made what I thought was a strong effort at getting through your book, but I seemed to be constantly interrupted by more, let us say, lively concerns.

CG: It is a complicated and time-consuming book for most. What problems did you personally have with it?

J: Well, for a psychologist you seem to have a very philosophical bent. That in itself makes warming up to your work somewhat difficult for me. I suppose I value things said a little more simply and crisply. Half the time I just couldn't follow you. And I really didn't get the feeling that you were that keen on keeping me around if I could.

Perhaps, too, my reaction has something to do with that subrole of scientist which I think you try to favor in your work, but never quite pull off. Actually, I could not make up my mind if this quality of yours was your special brand of intellectual razzle-dazzle, a kind of magic if you will, or maybe a literary fetish of some kind. I would like to believe what you say, that you have an empirical approach to your material, but you will forgive me if I say that I found you unconvincing on that point . . . I do not mean to be needlessly critical here.

CG: My approach is decidedly and quite self-consciously an empirical one. Perhaps you are simply intuiting the similarities between science and "magic" and finding those points of contact in my own work to be somewhat unsettling.

J: Ah! You wish to start out confusing me! You are calling attention to similarities that don't in fact exist. Science and magic have no more to do with each other than a cat does with the moon. Science is grounded in reality, is it not? Magic plays with illusion and superstition. Both have their respective merits and places in society. But, if you are in fact the scientist, I do not think you would want anyone to confuse you with being a magician. Or, perhaps more urgently put, to which doctor would you go to mend a broken leg? One who knows science or one who knows . . . witches?

CG: Oh, I believe it is a much more complicated problem than that. On your own initial proposition, may I ask you a question? You stated that science was grounded in reality. May I ask you whose reality are you referring to?

J: Ours, of course. Yours and mine. The reality that we share and live in. The real reality!

CG: So, you believe science goes about its business apart from the scientist who is busying himself, or from the tools he uses to keep himself busy?

J: Do you really want to squabble with me? You are going to become overly subtle now, as you do in your book, and painfully labor a point which, if it makes you happy, I'll gladly concede to you at the start. Listen, you do not have to convince me how you can maneuver an argument. I do not doubt that you are quite brilliant in your own weird way. I likewise should not have to tell you that intelligence is not the only factor running this world of ours. There is much flesh and blood that can't be twisted around or denied by mere intellection. You have to taste it and feel it to really get to know it. I believe I'm saying that science deals with that reality.

CG: I suppose you were looking then for something a little more gritty or definite in my book; something concrete that could be used in more unequivocal terms.

J: Of course!

CG: Well, that is in my book too . . . but it all wears an unfamiliar face to you.

J: I am trying to be open-minded here, but you are making it very difficult.

CG: You should be open at both ends . . . You must let go as well as take in. Perhaps you are too stuffed with old notions of reality? Perhaps you could evaluate some of your assumptions?

J: I will tell you frankly that you probably started off with one mark against you even before I started your book. But I think now you have clinched it. You consider yourself part of a profession which cares about people, but look how crude and insulting you've become. Where are your sensitivities, man! Talk about my assumptions, would you! It has always bothered me how psychologists declare themselves experts on people's lives. The ones I have known are positively the least fit to advise others on problems of any kind, much less those concerning human relationships. You want assumptions? Try that one on for size.

CG: I would assure you I have had those exact same thoughts about my profession.

J: [long pause] . . . Is this your way of diffusing the hostilities and robbing me of my point?

CG: I am saying I share your suspicions and do not hold that against you in any way . . . But can I get you back to the topic of your reaction to my book?

J: At this stage, all I can give you is my gut feelings.

CG: I'm sure.

J: Well, perhaps if you were to have made a little better effort at making yourself more "readable," I could give you a better reaction. Anyway, so much of your typology seems concocted for its own sake. You overdo your analyses and end up overcomplicating matters to make everything fit what seems to be a very eccentric and preordained scheme. There's no room for people to breathe in your work. It's enough to give me fits! Your subtlety should be measured out more discriminately, I think.

CG: You've brought that point up before in another way. And listening to the problems it is causing you, I think the criticism has much substance to it. I, unfortunately for you, tend to view psychological reality as quite a subtle and paradoxical affair. I say so in a deliberate manner in many of my works. Furthermore, if people would bother to read my work with a little more care and deliberation, I think they would find my point of view quite clearly and persuasively presented, even given the complexity of the material I am dealing with. If it is any consolation to you, though, you may rest assured that I do not use paradox to escape reality . . . it is rather my starting point.

J: Doctor, you're becoming a bit defensive here, aren't you?

CG: A proper defense seems to be called for! Please do not believe that this business of being overly complicated or overly subtle is a position with which I will rest content. Nature, of course, is as complicated as anything we humans may imagine, and yet she goes on without nearly the fuss or anxiety that have become the hallmarks of our so-called sophisticated existence and progressive evolution. Why? It is precisely because nature does not overdo it! Modern man by comparison is everywhere outside and beyond himself! If my work has intended anything, it has been to clear up this awful and dangerous mess that modern man has gotten himself into by "overdoing it," as you say.

J: I have no idea what you are talking about! I get the feeling that at times you are ranting and raving like some wide-eyed oracle mistakenly placed at a McDonald's to catch the lunch crowd. No doubt now you will feel obliged to prove the merits of the confused statement you just made, a tactic which incidentally you overuse in your book. Let me talk on that a bit.

This need you have to *prove* everything makes me very uncomfortable. First, you make these outlandish comments and then you spend an inordinate and painful amount of time trying to prove what you said. Why not simply spare us the outlandish statements in the first place? I feel you are trying to involve me in some diabolical game in which you are the only one who knows the rules. This in effect allows you to declare what's real or acceptable or what is not.

In fact, I wonder if this need to prove everything is not also a "typical" trait of psychologists. So much of psychology generally seems to be built up around different psychologists' needs to document the invisible and then go on endlessly debating with each other on whether or not it whistles. And much of this activity no doubt is at the expense of their hardworking patients!

CG: My friend, you have gone from being defensive to being most offensive! Anyway, I suspect that we psychologists do spend more of our time on trying to understand our own lives than the average individual does, and this also involves our patients, as well as a certain level of argument and complexity that is not everyone's cup of tea.

I think too, however, that perhaps what you complain about has a positive side. At least in my case it does. I could never begin to apply or recommend my own work if I had not taken my experiments and observations far enough on myself. Paradoxically, you see, my problems as you describe them are my salvation . . . [Jabbok winces in exasperation].

At least you must agree with me that the more we psychologists work on these issues for ourselves, the less a nuisance we are likely to become to our patients and the less diabolical the effects would be on them as well . . . Still, I will grant you it is all a very tricky affair . . . [long pause].

J: [Observably, very restless] And what of the nuisance you have made of yourself today? You have aggravated an otherwise easygoing type of fellow.

CG: You are certainly that, though much more, as you have proven today as well.

J: [a lengthy pause] You do realize I mean no offense with you on these matters.

CG: No offense taken . . . I would appreciate it, though, if you would collect your thoughts for a moment and give me a summary statement about your reaction to my book on psychological types.

J: You are pushing your luck.

CG: Your opinion on this matter is worth much to me.

J: Well, as you can tell by now, I am not trained in your field, and neither want nor need to haunt the interior landscapes as you do. But, for whatever it's worth, I still feel you tend to overcomplicate matters. In fact, I feel you're something of a sophist. Why, I bet you could squirm your way out of almost anything. Also, you take a good thing, like imagination, and go too far with it, making it a confused and counterproductive mess. Plus, you don't seem to want to be understood by anybody outside your little coterie of followers. Who are you writing for anyway? As you know, or at least as I have said, there is a whole wide world out there, waiting to be lived in . . . not just thought about or reflected upon.

Why, as I look out of your window I can barely keep myself still long enough to finish talking with you. In fact, I am ready to bolt out of here and go for a good run. Why don't you join me? That's my kind of therapy, and it's free. Anyway, I just can't for the life of me figure out why you would want to spend so much time by yourself in some dank room with nothing but your pen, paper, and your idle speculations for company! You need to get out of that old writing chair and just throw yourself into life . . . then you will know what I am talking about.

CG: [pause] I wonder what you see out that window. You mentioned "throwing yourself into life . . . " I can see you are an enthusiastic and industrious person. But, do you not worry about the consequences of "throwing yourself into life" as you say? Do you often consider the effects of your actions?

J: Consider, yes. But, worry? Perhaps you should worry about the consequences of your not acting . . .

CG: The issue of course is to determine what kind of action the situation calls for. I think in most instances less trouble would be caused by not acting than by acting in an unreflective or unconscious manner. Often we compound our troubles by doing more and listening less . . . [pause] We must learn again to listen to the sources of our inner nature and correctly interpret their urgings and origins . . . don't you think?

J: [mystified quiet]

CG: So, sir, you see I do agree with you: it is time to act. But, I speak now of true action for the individual concerned, and not action for action's sake, or simply to advance the mob. True action listens and evaluates based on all the significant information given one in one's situation. True action is conscious action.

And, so too, sir, you must see now that what I do in my writing and in my work is the truth that is given me to "do." Such is my "action." Even my typology, which you found so disagreeable, is a "doing," an attempt in fact to help to get you to your own true way of "doing," or perhaps better, "being."

J: You are beginning to sound something like an old philosopher talking to himself. But, I understand your sympathies. In fact, I like you most when you take such pleading tones.

CG: Pleading tones? That is disturbing! I did not realize I was pleading. Perhaps you may spare me such compliments and finish your summary.

J: My, you are a thick-skinned and scrappy sort of fellow. I will oblige you just to finish this off. I sense you need to scale down your work to a more tolerable and accessible level. You know, frankly I have never even heard of Carl Spitteler or any of a half dozen other people you mention in your book. Bring in your reach, for Pete's sake. Get back down to earth. Get back to the simple things. Maybe even stop reading and writing for a while. Develop a hobby that will take you outside of yourself and preferably get you involved with some people other than the kind you are accustomed to.

In a humanities course I took in college years ago, I remember finding out that Francisco Petrarca, the father of the Renaissance, mind you, had only a couple hundred books in his entire library. I bet you read that many books in one year! Actually, you can only read one book at a time, and even if you read one a day every day for the rest of your life, you'll never really be done, will you? And how much of each book do you really remember?

Finally, when it comes down to it, how much fun can you be having pursuing these obsessions of yours? Listen to me, do yourself and everyone around you a big favor: see how good you have it, and leave well enough alone. Then decide on something you can do that will really have a positive effect on your fellowman. You know, I think that is actually what you want, isn't it? And, incidentally, I believe that is a most admirable goal and that you truly are a man up to the challenge.

CG: [laughing] You show excellent insight into how a large part of the real world operates.

J: It is not a bad world.

CG: [still laughing] It's frightening . . . Nonetheless, I hope we will be seeing more of each other while we are inhabiting it. I think even this brief exchange had its high points.

J: I agree. And, I am sure we will be seeing more of each other. I have just moved into the neighborhood.

Now, what are we to make of this little excursus? First, an almost infinite number of characters, words, and situations can be generated when a finite set of typological "rules" are loosely kept in mind and applied and one allows the energy to "flow." Generating this kind of interaction then gives us new information.

Second, whatever inhibitions one may have as an author in creating a typological dialogue, the opportunity to read back into any dialogue or actual conversation and interpret examples of typological "facts" seems likewise unlimited. We can look at what is going on in terms of typological patterns.

Third, while the dialogue is ideally contrived to demonstrate the two opposing psychological types interacting on a specific topic, one can readily see how using one's imagination can help to realize typological patterns as they may occur in any conversation on virtually any issue or concern. It is then possible to refine one's understanding as one stays attentive (listens) to how an individual personality actually does or does not flesh out a particular psychological type.

Fourth, we must concede the fact that one can generate legitimate criticisms of Jung's work by applying Jung's typology to itself—Jabbok does make several legitimate criticisms of Jung's work.

Barbara Hannah comments that after Jung had written *Psychological Types*, "Jung was able to speak the 'language' of every type. Just as he took a lot of trouble to learn the languages of his patients (English, French, etc.), so he learned to put things into the language of the psychological type to whom he was talking" (1976, p. 133). We may, of course, assume that Jung himself would have communicated somewhat better with a potential adversary than he did in our dialogue.

However, this does not take anything away from the confrontation of the two types over the matter of Jung's work. In fact, theoretically it would be possible to imaginatively move around in any of the sixteen psychological types to find particular vantage points from which to criticize Jung's work.

When reviewing Jabbok's comments in particular, we must realize that his psychological type was the most extreme typological example of the possibilities available to oppose Jung's psychological type, and would therefore pose special problems of understanding. One would, for example, expect the two types to "talk past" one another as much as they did, since they represent to each other the least familiar aspects of their respective psychological types. For example, we see in our dialogue that Jung finds it next to impossible to get some cogent criticism from Jabbok concerning the ideas in his book (a need of Jung's extraverted thinking). On the other hand, Jabbok, speaking often as the voice of humanity, seems hell-bent on reintegrating Jung into the mainstream of life. Any criticism he does make of Jung's book is based on such a mission.

In turn, though, Jung shies away from playing into Jabbok's hands and does not develop the conversation with the simplicity for which Jabbok himself is pleading. Jung prefers a complex and individual outlook on practically everything that comes up in the conversation, except concerning complexity and individuality themselves, which would involve him in a logical contradiction. To Jabbok, Jung's oxymoronic philosophy appears as "simply complex" and "individually universal," and frustratingly so. For Jung, he could not be otherwise.

Both perspectives are consistent with the two psychological types as one may imagine them. Furthermore, because both types are so removed from or "foreign" to one another, one can more dramatically see and appreciate the points made in the discussion. Finally, with typology we have a way of viewing opposition and difference as a means to see the many sides of an issue, which is in turn an aid in achieving a more objective understanding of the matter at hand. Imagine the individual who is well equipped with the gamut of typological perspectives, building his or her life with such a "psychology of consciousness."

We will leave our two types now, not wanting to resolve the opposition, but rather to recognize and appreciate their different perspectives within this larger typological context. Through these two competitive points of view, each has become more interesting and meaningful than either one could be on its own.

Note

1. In the analysis of Jung's type which follows, I am aware that I am going up against Jung's own self-understanding. This would be

utter folly and arrogance without some explanation. Jung understood himself to be introverted thinking with strong intuition. I have struggled with the question of Jung's type for over a decade, imagining him in dialogue with his typological opposite using a number of different typological perspectives. Whether what follows is "true" or "true enough," I leave for the discerning reader to decide. Jung just may have been a strange enough bird to have two superior functions working in both attitudes. Let the debate continue.

IV

The Strange Case of the Inferior Function

Just as there is no energy without the tension of opposites, so there can be no consciousness without the perception of differences.

(CW 14, para. 603)

DIFFERENCES ARE NECESSARY and unavoidable. We may not always know precisely or ultimately what all these differences mean; indeed, their meanings may change over time. But that differences are essential for orientation and consciousness is beyond question.

Yet differences in and of themselves are alarming and strange. If all we had available to orient ourselves were facts of dissimilarities and distinctions, our situation would prove desperate. Having everything different is as bad as having everything the same, the former akin to being lost in a large city, the latter akin to being lost at sea. In fact, it would seem that we learn first by making the strange into the familiar, into what we think we "know." We try to find the familiar in the strange, the similarities in the differences.

Typology would have us believe that we learn about our individual or personal selves in just such a manner, first looking at and getting to know what has become most familiar to ourselves about ourselves, and then later moving into the stranger domains of our personality in terms of such familiarities.

Often, movement into the stranger parts of our personality, when it does occur, is quite unnerving, to say the least, and reason enough to give us pause. The familiar parts of our personality are often not up to the task. Just when we think we are getting to know ourselves, it is as if the strange parts take over, forcing us into the mysteries of our psyche as a whole.

But even in such moments of introspection or reflection, we still seem to seek solace and insight from that part of our personality that we deem most "like" us, most reliable. Just as in times of trouble we may go to a good and trusted friend for sympathy and understanding, we come to count on those friendly and reliable parts of our personality to get us through any trouble we may be facing. It is hard for us to reverence the mystery of who we are, to reverence the "strange."

For purposes of our study now, these friendly and reliable parts of our personality would be represented by the conscious side of our own psychological type. As such, a person's psychological type serves the individual as an integrated way to maintain good relations with both the internal and external worlds. However, as we will see, serious problems can come with seemingly unalloyed success.

Consciousness itself is a broader concept than an individual's psychological type, as is the notion of one's total personality. Yet the conscious side of a person's psychological type is often such a good and useful representation of how we function in the everyday world that we tend to separate it from the whole of our personality, clean it up along the way, and finally take it to be our true and good self, the reward of our efforts to date, the center of our being. Life itself becomes simply a matter of doing what we can and must to "keep a good thing going."

When this psychological posture is assumed, it becomes easier to ignore or avoid what is unfamiliar, least like us, least friendly, or least reliable within our own personality. As a consequence, the differences within a personality often become competitive with a person's conscious psychological type. As such, just as the "strange" is trying to break into consciousness, it is pushed more and more to the periphery of consciousness or beyond.

In a therapeutic setting, the problem of differences is invariably somewhere in the picture. In some cases a person will need to experience him- or herself as capable of functioning in the world in a characteristic manner, to take measures to help put specific differences together in such a way that the individual may acknowledge and develop his or her own psychological type in a unique and conscious manner.

In other instances, a person's psychological type has already been differentiated and has, in a sense, taken over consciousness at the expense of the unconscious. It is then that the strange and the unfamiliar, which lies within one's psychological type but outside immediate consciousness, can become problematic.

Between the two extremes there are countless degrees and variations concerning how well or how poorly a person relates to his or her own psychological type. Most commonly, individuals have intentions to consolidate the conscious side of their respective psychological types, but find a weakened form of the inferior function getting in the way. These cases, while troublesome, are manageable and usually shortterm. They are also the least enlightening concerning how the inferior function can operate when it is in full pitch.

The problem of the inferior function is best understood by looking at the person who in fact has developed the conscious side of his or her particular psychological type and is beginning to experience eruptions from the unconscious in a negative way. That is to say, the inferior function as such becomes a serious therapeutic problem usually after a person has achieved a differentiated psychological type, and in the process has effectively separated or divided his or her own personality into the combative realms of conscious and unconscious life (the good and the bad, the familiar and the strange, the known and the unknown).

Such a person sooner or later will have to contend with the feeling of being peculiarly separate or divided from him- or herself, a psychological problem that is the modern equivalent of being cast out of the Garden of Eden for the second time. When this happens, consciousness will eventually be presented with the new and difficult task of handling what has happened to the personality "in exile." Failing that, the individual will regress to earlier, more nondifferentiated stages of development. The inferior function, in its most animalistic or barbaric form, then can and will take over.

In typological development, there is a deadly risk that when one does not move forward at the right time, one falls back. Depending on the severity of the split between consciousness and the unconscious, outside professional help may be necessary to keep the individuation process moving in a natural manner. In this sense, helping an individual to change and grow within the larger context of his or her life is a challenging and important task for the creative therapist.

Jung's typological approach to this problem of being "thrown out" of oneself begins by calling our direct attention to the quality of the relationship that we have with those neglected parts of our own personalities, what Jung often terms the inferior side of our psychological type. In fact, as we will see, it is the inferior function itself that often operates in each person's psychological type as both the lure and the trigger that ultimately throws an individual into a new experience of consciousness as such.

In this chapter, we will first examine the inferior function as a theoretical issue. While much of this initial material may prove somewhat tedious and the terminology cumbersome, it is intended to fine-tune some of the typological concepts and guidelines we have discussed so far. We will also give a general narrative of an extreme case in which the inferior function and shadow have taken over the superior function and ego to the point where a change in consciousness becomes necessary.

In that it represents the dark side of our psychological types, the inferior function has much to do with how we treat one another and how we view the world. In section two of this chapter, we will see how and why this is the case. This involves us in an excursus into the importance of the inferior function as a moral issue, a topic which may seem to go well beyond typology proper. Nonetheless, it is a sufficiently important issue to warrant discussing the inferior function in this context. As one becomes more and more familiar with how powerfully the inferior function plays out in the collective, one feels more and more compelled to address this issue in terms of its social and ethical consequences.

The Inferior Function and Typological Theory

Both the schema below and on page 81 are based on a diagram used by Marie-Louise von Franz in her series of lectures/ essays on the inferior function (initially presented at the Jung Institute in Zürich in 1961). The schemata are intended to serve as a summary and review of Jung's typological theory as we have come to know it in this study. They will also serve as a means to highlight the relative "place" of the inferior function as a starting point for our analysis. Von Franz's original diagram, along with her comments on the inferior function, can be found in *Lectures on Jung's Typology* (1984). Direct mention is made of her work with the inferior function now, because it is easily the most compelling and poignant psychological treatment of the subject since Jung's own writings.

Typological Schema for Any *Introverted* Type

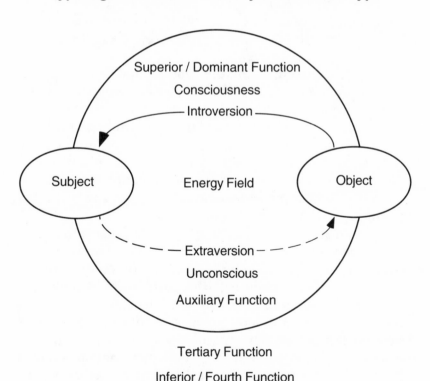

This schema is useful for a number of reasons. The solid curved arrow illustrates the flow of energy at the conscious level being withdrawn from the object to the subject (introversion); the dotted curved arrow indicates the counter-movement of energy at the unconscious level, from the subject to the object (extraversion). Thus we have already visually established the dynamic principles behind Jung's typological theory.

In addition, the hierarchical representation of the four functions allows us to locate where the four functions "stand" in relationship to consciousness. The superior or primary function at the top of the diagram is the most differentiated function in consciousness, most characteristic and most under the control of the personality. The inferior function at the foot of the diagram (outside the circle) would be the least characteristic and least under the control of the personality. Jung describes it as "undomesticated, unadapted, uncontrolled, and primitive." Most tellingly he adds, " . . . *because of its contamination with the collective unconscious, it possesses archaic and mystical qualities, and is the complete opposite of the most differentiated function"* (CW 11, para. 184, italics mine).

The circle encompassing the superior and auxiliary functions signifies the individual's manageable inner and outer worlds. Within that circle/world, a psychological type would have a "lead" or superior function that would be characterized by confidence and self-assurance, and an auxiliary or "helper" function that is slightly unconscious, usually operating in the opposite attitude to the superior function but nonetheless accessible and useful to the person in his or her daily life.

It should also be recalled from Chapter II that if the superior function were a perceiving or irrational function (either sensation or intuition), then the auxiliary function would be a judging or rational function (either thinking or feeling); conversely, if the superior function were a judging or rational function, then the auxiliary function would be a perceiving or irrational function. The overall effect on the participating personality represented by the circle in our diagram is one of relative balance between introversion and extraversion, the irrational/perceiving and rational/judging functions, and, to some degree, consciousness and the unconscious.

A similar schema for extraverted types would look like this:

Typological Schema for Any *Extraverted* Type

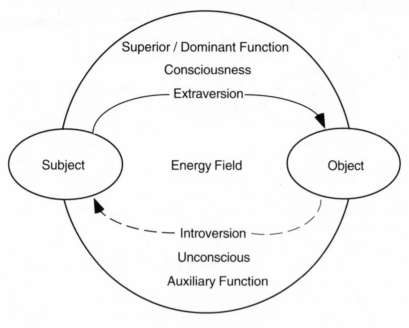

Superior / Dominant Function

Consciousness

Extraversion

Subject   Energy Field   Object

Introversion

Unconscious

Auxiliary Function

Tertiary Function

Inferior / Fourth Function

In comparing the two schemata, one should notice that the extravert will have to contend with his (or her) auxiliary, tertiary, and inferior functions through an unconscious introversion. Meanwhile, the introvert has to handle his (or her) auxiliary, tertiary, and inferior functions through an unconscious extraversion. Because of the latter, introverts may customarily seem more "out of line" or "out of step" with the outer world; i.e., much of the introvert's struggle and discomfort with the three functions take place in contention with the outer world. By contrast, the extravert's problems with the auxiliary, tertiary, and inferior functions take place for the most part out of public view. Consistent with common observations, then, introverts generally seem less confident than extraverts in their dealings with the outer world.

It should be noted also from our diagrams that the tertiary and inferior functions are conspicuously out of range of the main activity taking place in the conscious personality of both introverts and extraverts, i.e. they are "out of the circle." In both schemata, all functions that fall below consciousness are commonly understood by Jung as inferior functions. This would include even the auxiliary function, if that function were not sufficiently differentiated and available to consciousness.

In one sense, by "inferior" Jung simply means to designate a quality of relation between consciousness and the unconscious. It follows that if the superior or primary function is the most conscious and differentiated function in the personality, the other three functions (the auxiliary, tertiary, and fourth functions) are relatively less so, meaning "inferior" by comparison to the "superior" function. These other functions therefore share a quality of relative "inferiority" with one another.

However, Jung draws heavily on the word "inferior" when he interchangeably uses it to indicate specifically the fourth or "most inferior" of the four functions. In our schemata, this fourth function can be seen as the farthest away from consciousness, the most difficult to "get to," looking down from the top.

Jung also relies heavily on the word "auxiliary," by which he not only means the "second best" function available to the conscious personality, but likewise the third or tertiary function. If the tertiary function is sufficiently differentiated to be useful to consciousness, then indeed we may consider it as an "auxiliary," or helping, function. However, this is almost never the case.

Jung does not use the term "tertiary function" in his book on psychological types. I am using the designation of "tertiary" over "auxiliary" for two reasons. First, I believe Jung intends to draw our attention to something rather specific when he uses the term "auxiliary function," namely that function which complements the superior function in consciousness. In that sense, the "tertiary" function is rarely "auxiliary," i.e. helpful or assisting. Second, using the term "tertiary" to designate the third function will allow us to more properly view this function in tandem with the inferior or fourth function. Together, the tertiary and inferior functions act as distinguishing features through which the shadow archetype emerges from the unconscious into consciousness. The *shadow* is that archetypal image or personification that in Jung's general psychology represents the most despised and neglected parts of our personality; we have also referred to aspects of it from a typological point of view as one's counter-personality.

We may make a further point in regard to the ongoing process of differentiating the functions that in essence will take us into the heart of the individuation process itself. Most individuals have a difficult time getting any function to act on their behalf. We do exceptionally well to get the dominant and auxiliary functions up to consciousness. Once this is done, one may properly speak of the conscious side of an individual's psychological type as being functionally "in place," useful to the ego and consciousness, and fairly representative of the person's everyday personality.

While the tertiary function can be brought into consciousness, it most commonly stays down in the unconscious with the inferior function, where it shares in its power. The inferior function draws its power from the unconscious itself, and as such can never be pulled up to consciousness. In von Franz's phrasing, "the fish is too big for the rod" (1984, p. 17). Because of this, the inferior function in typology is the true and distinguishing nexus between consciousness and the unconscious, a key facet of the individuation process itself, and we will view it as such. Jung goes so far as to say, "It is precisely the least valued function that enables life, which was threatened with extinction by the differentiated function, to continue" (CW 6, para. 444).

However, before looking more closely at the fourth function in this regard, some further comments on the tertiary function itself are necessary. In my research on typology, I have not been able to find anything specifically written on the tertiary function, at least as we are now using that term. The comments that follow draw on the richness and suggestiveness of Jung's theory, along with my own typological observations of clients and individuals.

A person who introverts his superior function and extraverts his auxiliary function (i.e., any introvert) has, typologically speaking, an extraverted tertiary function and an extraverted inferior function. Should this introvert rely heavily on his (or her) auxiliary function by often pulling it up to consciousness for competent use, the tertiary function (also extraverted) becomes all the more neglected and left to the unconscious. This creates the proverbial tension between opposites (in typological theory, it will be remembered that the auxiliary function is always opposite to the tertiary function just as the superior function is always opposite to the inferior function).

In my observations and experience, it is not uncommon for introverts especially to develop their extraverted auxiliary function to the point where the tension between the auxiliary and tertiary function is as extreme as that between the superior and inferior functions. The tertiary function then becomes highly problematic (more unconscious) for the introvert as its polar opposite (the auxiliary function) becomes more and more differentiated in consciousness. In effect, this movement of energy toward consciousness makes the tertiary function closer in kind and nature to the inferior function than it would be to the auxiliary function. Though the "ranking" of the functions does not say so directly, from the perspective of consciousness this would translate "three is closer to four than two," i.e., the tertiary function is closer to the inferior function than it is to the auxiliary.

A concrete example of the above would be as follows: a person who introverts his superior feeling function and extraverts his auxiliary intuitive function (an introverted feeling-type with intuition) has, typologically speaking, an extraverted sensing (tertiary) function and an extraverted thinking (inferior) function. Should this introvert overdevelop or overdifferentiate his auxiliary intuitive function (a common practice among introverts in adapting to the world), his extraverted tertiary sensing function can become highly problematic. Such a person often has a hopelessly bad sense of direction, may neglect his body (not exercise or eat too much), lack an eye for details, not be at all mechanically inclined, have a poor memory, be stingy, be unnecessarily pessimistic, and on the whole be out of step with "consensus reality."

For extraverts, the tertiary function can be equally problematic, though less commonly so due to the fact that
extraverts are less inclined to overdevelop their auxiliary
function than are introverts. Nonetheless, for extraverts, an
example of a tertiary function eliding with the inferior function and the unconscious is as follows: a person who
extraverts her superior thinking function and introverts her
auxiliary sensing function (an extraverted thinking-type with
sensing) has, typologically speaking, an introverted intuitive
(tertiary) function and an introverted feeling (inferior) function. Should this extravert overdevelop her auxiliary sensing
function, her introverted (tertiary) intuitive function can
become extremely troublesome. Such a person often has personal "superstitions" that cannot be violated, dark prophe-
cies, jags of irrationality and suspicion, and a vivid dream-
life; may appear fanatical in her beliefs; and have serious
difficulties getting "the big picture."

In both our cases, the tertiary functions are highly primitive or undifferentiated in form and coloration, a result of
their close affiliation with the unconscious and the inferior
function. In fact, in many instances the tertiary function
could be thought of as the inferior function's "helper," an
"auxiliary" function for the counter-personality constellated
in the unconscious, while the inferior function would itself
be considered the "lead" or "superior" function (CW 6, para.
670). It is at this point that the shadow archetype may utilize
both the tertiary and inferior functions and take on actual
characteristics of the person's counter-personality or alter-
ego.

If we have understood the relative place and power of the
tertiary function so far (and not been totally defeated by typological language), we are ready to move on specifically to how
the inferior function may operate in the personality. Just as
the tertiary function has considerable power as a result of the
tension created between it and the auxiliary function, the
inferior function has immense power created by the opposition of consciousness and the unconscious. Due to this
excess of tension, when one truly meets the inferior function
in all its force, von Franz refers to the encounter as "the great
conflict" (1984, p. 17).

To understand the significance of "the great conflict," we

must work through a certain semantic boggle with the word "inferior." Because consciousness cannot do what it wants with the inferior function, it often views it as "weak," or as a kind of "misfit function." Our characterization of this function as "inferior" reveals the bias of approaching material from the unconscious with a "psychology of consciousness."

However, only from a typological egocentrism could we consider the inferior function "weak" in any simple sense. From the point of view of the overall personality, the fact that the inferior function cannot fit into the parameters of the normal functioning ego indicates only that a "larger" and more ominous entity, of which the inferior function itself is only a part, may be "pulling the strings."

The other two "inferior" functions (the auxiliary and tertiary) are at least theoretically capable of being differentiated and brought into consciousness. But the fourth or "true" inferior function remains loyal to the unconscious throughout the individuation process. As such, it is an eloquent if unnerving testimony that there is more to one's personality than meets the eye. Von Franz comments, "You can never rule or educate [the inferior function] or make it act as you would like" (1984, p. 19). Indeed, the opposite is often the case: the inferior function "rules and educates" you, from a vantage point that confounds and dwarfs the conscious, everyday personality. When Jung tells us that the inferior function is "contaminated" by all elements of both the personal and collective unconscious, and for this reason has "archaic and mystical qualities" (CW 11, para. 184), one begins to get an idea of what the individual has to deal with when the inferior function comes into play.

In a telling metaphor borrowed from Jung, von Franz calls the inferior function the "door through which all the figures of the unconscious come into consciousness." She adds, "our conscious realm is like a room with four doors, and it is the fourth door by which the shadow, the animus or the anima, and the personification of the Self come in" (1984, p. 54). One could stretch the metaphor even further and say that whatever is behind the first three doors that one opens, consciousness can handle more or less on its own terms; but the fourth door is often experienced as a trap-door leading to parts and places as yet unknown. The contents behind the fourth door are then often beyond the ego's normal scope of integration.

Because the inferior function is to such an extent connected with the unconscious, it makes sense to view it through images and metaphors, the language of the unconscious. The most common metaphor for the inferior function is arrived at through realizing its nature in opposition and contrast to the superior function. If the superior function in consciousness can be understood as the metaphoric "light of day," as is certainly plausible, then the inferior function in the unconscious is the metaphoric "dark of night." As such, Jung concludes, "the inferior function is practically identical with the dark side of the human personality" (CW 9i, para. 222).

When all the above activity is antagonistically stirred up in the psyche (when the superior function opposes the inferior function, consciousness opposes the unconscious, or analogously, when light opposes dark, when good opposes evil, when right opposes wrong, when order opposes chaos), one can immediately sense that life itself becomes "charged" with a kind of energy that turns mere existence into high drama.

Often, out of an individual's compelling sense to "be strong," "be right," " be good," "be noble," "be normal," or "be in control," the conscious side of the person's psychological type is reinforced and brought to bear upon the unsettling eruptions from the other side, the unconscious. What the inferior function is bringing to consciousness is then either denied or projected onto the external world. This situation not only results in continued suffering for the individual and more repeated assaults by the inferior function; it also can cause serious problems for others as well.

If the individual's need to maintain a superior stance against the inferior function is extreme, those around him become scapegoats assigned to carry his own dark side for him. When a person projects the negative contents of the unconscious in this manner, naturally all kinds of damage are possible. The unconscious is cut loose from the conscious personality and thrown out into the world as if it were a power on its own. Normal behavior is circumvented, laws undermined. Anything or anyone that happens to fit the

needs of the person in conflict may become an occasion for
ritually acting out in reality what otherwise may have been
handled by a conscious relationship with the unconscious.

Very often projection of this kind gives an individual time
to retrench and regroup. When one is projecting the negative
aspects of one's personality, it gives one a false sense of security and power. Each time, almost imperceptibly, the individual is giving more and more of his or her personality over to
the unconscious, becoming more and more accustomed to
dealing with life in a negative and unconscious manner. Projections can go on forever in this negative form, with the
gradual erosion of the ego being the costly price one pays, not
to mention the harm done to others. Any person could feasi-
bly find the needed scapegoats that would make life an
unending series of negative but nonetheless sustaining experiences.

The question of suffering brought on by the inferior function projected in negative forms brings to mind the problem
of the inferior function as a moral issue. This problem is of
such great importance that it warrants extensive and separate
treatment in section two of this chapter. There we will have
to examine in finer detail what the unconscious itself is like
and how it may affect society at large.

In the meantime, we will focus on what happens in an
extreme case in which the inferior function, representing the
unconscious, comes into direct contact with an individual's
constricting psychological type. Though the following narrative is somewhat general in tone, it relates to a very profound
and personal experience that any individual may go through
in one degree or another at special times in his or her life,
especially when he or she thinks they "know it all."

When the inferior function is warring inside the personality at full pitch, whatever the superior function has prided
itself on most will be eventually "taken over" by the dark
side of the personality. If the person's superior function is
thinking, inferior feeling will dominate, making the person
appear overly sensitive, sentimental, and lost to subjectivity
and self-doubt; if the person's superior function is intuition,
inferior sensation will dominate, rendering the person confused or absent-minded about facts and figures, and out of
step with everyday reality.

The conscious superior function is in fact no match for any unconscious inferior function. The dark side of the personality soon eclipses the ego, which is left with little but the pretense of its functional worth and well-being. The personality appears to others as "crazy." One can even use typology in this way to describe the different styles of "craziness" that encroach on normal functioning psychological types, as von Franz has done in her work on the inferior function (1984, pp. 38–53).

Regardless of the particulars, in all extreme cases when the inferior function is truly at work, it falsifies the superior function and tyrannizes the personality until the person wants literally "to crawl out of his own skin," or even to die. This, mind you, is only the trouble going on in the internal world.

Against continued negative projected contents of the unconscious in the external world, the person soon fails to be able to tell the difference between friend and foe, contending with the ever-present adversary he or she always seems to be finding. In the extreme, the world itself becomes a Machiavellian nightmare from which the person cannot awake.

The overall effect on the conscious personality is that the inferior function has turned strength into weakness, right into wrong, good into evil, nobility into disgrace, normalcy into insanity, control into chaos, certainty into suspicion, confidence into doubt. It has done this by allowing the full weight of the unconscious to move in on the unsuspecting psychological type.

At the stage in a person's life when the inferior function is making an unrelenting attack to break up the ego or get consciousness to acknowledge the unconscious, dreams can be most revealing. The unconscious personification called the shadow generally now makes its appearance (CW 9ii, paras. 13–19). Jung considers the shadow an autonomous complex that often appears in dreams as a personality of the same sex as the dreamer. For males, this figure is typically a coward, murderer, bum, rapist, beggar, or any other detestable figure which can suitably flesh out the counter-personality of the individual type in question. For females, the shadow may be represented as a prostitute, a "little" or weak woman, a gypsy, or a deformed or retarded female. For both male and female, the shadow will offset whatever has been taken up into consciousness in too one-sided or positive a manner.

By such images, one would believe that the shadow is either all or essentially negative. This is certainly how most "normal" people often feel its effects on consciousness. But the shadow is also indispensable in terms of the amount of energy it brings from the unconscious to the whole personality. The appearance of a shadow figure in dreams signals that the image-making powers of the unconscious have been fully and recognizably activated, and that the symbolic life of the person has been vivified. For Jung, getting in touch with one's symbolic life is part of finding the "gold in dark places."

Dreams are normally characterized by this translation of problematic life experiences into the language of metaphor and symbols. According to Jung, dreams function in this way to compensate both the nature and contents of consciousness. Through their presentation of such images back to consciousness, dreams can therefore give us a pure rendering of the psychic condition of the individual as a whole, provided, of course, one can relate to the images in a meaningful way. In this sense, the shadow represents a "plus" or "positive" that the total personality cannot be without. As we will see (Chapter V: section 3, *The Transcendent Function*), energy drawn from the tension of opposites can be used to help the development of the overall personality.

As the shadow continues to move into consciousness, led on by the inferior function and in many cases helped as well by the tertiary function, the conscious personality fights to "stay strong." This is usually done by continuing to develop the superior and auxiliary functions. Such action, oddly enough, is the source of the problem in the first place. As Jung comments, ". . . to the degree that the greater share of libido (q.v.) is taken up by the favored function, the inferior function undergoes a regressive development; it reverts to the archaic (q.v.) stage and becomes incompatible with the conscious, favored function" (CW 6, para. 764). It is at this point that the shadow itself may actually dominate the person's conscious psychological type and carry with it the full and disruptive weight of the unconscious itself.

Should the ego or consciousness finally be beaten, the shadow will have its revenge and drag down the personality into its own dark domain. This would be the equivalent of a "psychotic break," crippling the person's ability to function in the world. One recalls a line from the 107th Psalm:

> Some sat in darkness and deep gloom,
> bound fast in misery and iron.

Psalm 107:10

At many points during this drama, "the great conflict" could have been better handled. There are always several recognizable characteristics that a particular psychological type will display when trouble is brewing, signals from the unconscious that the inferior function is in fact making its assault. Von Franz calls special attention to the times when a person appears overly sensitive or infantile, "touchy," vulnerable, or foolish. She writes, "The inferior function and the sore spot are absolutely connected" (1984, p. 11).

At such times the unconscious is ready to be taken seriously by consciousness, if one so chooses. The time to turn one's attention to the unconscious occurs now, not when the battle is being played out at full pitch in the external world or when the inferior function has dragged the personality into internal chaos. One must learn to recognize the clues representative of the inferior function or the shadow and to stay in touch with the unconscious through relating to such signals.

With each new "blowup," consciousness asks itself, "do I go down into the unconscious to meet my inferior function or my shadow, or can I live without these parts of my personality?" Unfortunately, all too often the answer which the ego feels fitting to give is that not only can it live without these other aspects of the personality, it will make sure to do so. And so the drama continues. Von Franz calls this bantering about with the inferior function "getting into the hot bath only to jump out again" (1984, p. 66).

But can we be so hard on the ego for not wanting to be "burned?" We have seen that from the point of view of one's ego, avoiding the inferior function is a completely reasonable thing to do. Because one spends most of one's time building up the superior function in consciousness (and perhaps the auxiliary function as well), it is crazy to think that we must give extra attention to the inferior function, the trouble-maker of the lot. Because one's experience with the inferior function is so often negative and disagreeable, an individual naturally finds him- or herself in the habit of not trusting the inferior function, of keeping it at arm's length.

Yet because the inferior function is such a key part of the individuation process itself, it simply cannot be left out of consideration without doing harm to the overall personality. There will, in fact, be certain periods in one's life when one can almost be sure of having to confront it: when the superior function in consciousness has reached its zenith, when the individual has become "bored" with himself, when the superior function confronts a problem that it is ill-equipped to solve, when you encounter the same inferior function playing out in someone else, at midlife . . . when major psychological shifts in one's typology take place, when one questions if there is anything more to life, when a person's psychological type has been sealed off from the unconscious, and when things are going "too well." In all these cases we have the potential for "the great conflict."

What can we say to the person in any of these situations, or to the person who continually misses the clues that the unconscious has been giving along the way, and ends up suffering the consequences? In a real sense, there is no good advice. One may be inclined to tell the person to "be strong," but that could be part of the problem. Or one may tell the person to "pray that God will help you," but that could be part of the problem. Or one may recommend that he talk to his therapist . . . but alas, that could be part of the problem as well. The person at the impasse is, finally, alone, save for the company of the inferior function (or shadow) itself. In this situation, the good therapist helps best by not helping at all. "Doing" or "prescribing" at such a point will rob the individual of what has taken him or her a lifetime to arrive at. As the client comes closer to the unconscious, both the therapist and the client alike do best to be still and look and listen. This is a threshold experience or liminal state for both client and therapist, not at all easy for either one to bear. But, it is here and now when what has to happen will happen.

Returning to the metaphor of the door, Jung writes:

For what comes after the door is, surprisingly enough, a boundless expanse full of unprecedented uncertainty, with apparently no inside and no outside, no above and no below, no here and no there, no mine and no thine, no good and no bad. It is the world of water, where all life floats in suspension; where the realm of the sympathetic system, the soul of everything living, begins: where I am indivisively this *and* that; where I experience the other in myself, and the other-than-myself experiences me. (CW 9i, para. 45)

One could not judge this type of experience as good or bad. It simply is a description of a person coming into contact with the reality of the psyche. As such, each person who has this experience has a different way of talking about it, if it can be talked about at all. What does become obvious, however, is that a person who undergoes such an ordeal changes in a very fundamental way. The individual no longer looks at him- or herself or the world quite the same way. Fortunately, some poets are especially helpful in conveying what happens. For example, Rainer Maria Rilke speaks about the experience in a poignant manner in his poem "Moving Forward":

The deep parts of my life pour onward,
as if the river shores were opening out.
It seems that things are more like me now
that I can see farther into paintings.

With my senses, as with birds, I climb
into the windy heaven, out of the oak,
and in the ponds broken off from the sky
my feeling sinks, as if standing on fishes.

The fifteenth-century Indian mystic poet Kabir simply says:

Something inside me
    has reached to the place
    where the world is breathing.

It seems that after a person has truly confronted the inferior function, such an experience is possible. Once the battle has run its course and the individual has faced the disowned parts of his or her personality, the tension between the conscious and unconscious parts of the personality gives way and the surplus energy begins to reveal the hidden contents of the unconscious itself. Perhaps from the few with the precious gift to tell about what is on the other side, we may gather up some courage to experience it for ourselves.

We will have occasion to come back to both Rilke and Kabir when we discuss, in Chapter V, the subject of the archetypal Self, the center or coordinating archetype of the psyche. For now, we need to see that the inferior function gives typological theory its teeth. Without the inferior function, typology could still be misread as too formal and abstract a model of individual development; the individuation process itself could appeal gutted and drawn. Such a misreading would go something like this: we are conceived in the image of a certain psychological type, "forget" it at birth, grope toward it in early childhood, test parts of it in adolescence, combine parts of it in adulthood, grope toward other parts of it at midlife, and put the whole thing together during old age. From this statement, one gets the impression that we are no longer the true subjects of our own fate. "Groping" toward "it" suggests a kind of dumb luck and lack of purpose; "it" is life lacking both adventure and the adventurer. But when the inferior function enters the picture, typological theory itself becomes invigorated, alive.

Because of what the inferior function is capable of opening us up to, we also realize that whatever problems the inferior function may cause us, they are problems that somehow we "deserve," not in the sense of punishment, but rather because we are personally *entitled* to them; they rightfully belong to us as a constitutive part of our individuality and being-in-the-world. They lead us to our unconscious life. This realization is close to Nietzsche's notion of *amor fati,* or love of one's own destiny.

It is actually an odd thought: to want to have our own problems. Is not happiness thought of by most as a problem-free existence? Do not many of us do everything in our power to be happy in this sense? Yet, as Aniela Jaffé comments, "individuation is always as much a fatality as a fulfillment" (1984, p. 83). We would add that the individuation process is itself often problematic, fitful, disturbing, avenging, violent, and ugly, because of the inferior function.

One can see here that Jung's typology is not simply

responsible, it is therapeutically provocative. *In extremis*, the neurotic gives us insight into the hidden attraction that the inferior function has for each of us. By showing us the tenacious hold which he keeps on his or her own problems, the neurotic reveals a kind of cryptic awareness that illness somehow signifies a part of his true identity. Such an intimation may be "abnormal" to all "normal" people who know better, but if you are a therapist (or simply a good friend), it is never quite so simple.

In every illness and every psychological problem there exists an uncanny truth and power having to do with the individual's full character and destiny. To be brought into a relationship with that aspect of an individual's life, whether as therapist, friend, or most importantly, within the context of one's own personality, is a psychological event of the first order.

We are not alone in treating the inferior function in the manner we have so far. Those following Jung have been equally forceful about the importance of the inferior function in regard to both Jung's typology as well as his overall psychology. In his book *The Symbolic Quest*, Edward Whitmont states, "There is no individuation, no 'becoming what we are,' unless we recognize and relate to the inferior function" (1978, p. 146). In a sense, Whitmont's insight fine-tunes Meier's belief, discussed earlier, that the individuation process begins and ends with typology (see p. 23).

Marie-Louise von Franz says the same thing in a different but as bold a manner when she claims that the inferior function "holds the secret key to the unconscious totality of the person" (1984, p. 7). Here von Franz is saying, in effect, that the inferior function holds the secret key to Jung's psychology as a whole, a notion we will explore in more detail in Chapter V.

However, what we must do next in this chapter is to take a step back and look more closely at how the inferior function may affect the social and cultural worlds of our modern civilization through the psychological mechanism of projection. Such experiences as both Rilke and Kabir describe are not inevitabilities in our everyday world; one does not simply pay one's dues and then get overwhelmed by the pleroma to live happily ever after. Or, as Jung was fond of saying, "One does not individuate on Mt. Everest."

We are each drawn to one another in odd and cruel ways to work out our psychological problems, and the pain and suffering that we inflict on each other as a result of how poorly we relate to our own inferior function is indeed mind-boggling, if not actually heart-stopping. As we will see in the next section of this chapter, the inferior function will assure us that morality is never an issue one suffers alone, individuation is not individual indulgence, and character cannot be separated from personality.

The Inferior Function As a Moral Issue

We have seen that the inferior function puts Jung's theory of types in its most dramatic guise. It heats things up and agitates. It evokes from us a shudder, a sigh, and a gasp. The inferior function is our troublemaker. It confutes, refutes, and complicates. It flips things around and inside-out. It challenges whatever we have accomplished, mocks our savvy, takes our daily bread. It stops us in our tracks.

Perhaps what is most devastating to us, the inferior function acts in all these ways on its own. That is, the inferior function, along with its archetypal compatriot the shadow, can take on a kind of active and authoritative presence in our everyday lives. In its most diabolical aspects, it tampers with and sabotages our relationships, turning friend into foe, or intrapsychically speaking, Self into non-self. In the blink of an eye, the inferior function can go from a "what" to a "who," from you to your neighbor, from your neighbor back to you. Jung explains:

> The essence of the inferior function is autonomy. It is independent, it attacks, it fascinates, and so spins us about that we are no longer masters of ourselves and can no longer rightly distinguish between ourselves and others. (CW 7, para. 85)

Yet amidst all our trepidation, we would likewise be reminded by Jung that "it is necessary for the development of character that we should allow the other side, the inferior function, to find expression" (Ibid.). The ego asks why anyone in his or her right mind should actually allow the troublesome aspects of his or her personality to be expressed. Jung's answer is "for the development of character." This remark, less a warning than an evocation, is our motive for devoting special attention and a separate section to this strange part of Jung's typology. For Jung, the inferior function is thus not just a trouble-maker *extraordinaire*, it is a moral exigency as well.

Character, morality, and personality are all inextricably connected in Jung's psychology; they are all products of coming to terms with the energy of the psyche and the "fundamental laws of human nature" (CW 6, para. 356). However, unlike many moralists, Jung does not focus his attention on external laws, codes, or decrees as the primary sources of morality. That is, an individual's morality is not understood from the outside looking in, nor are character and personality ultimately judged or shaped by any outside authority. Rather, the roots of morality are posited inside one's own deepest nature as an individual; morality itself extends out from the person to the world.

In this way, a person's unconscious reliance on external laws, rules, and restrictions seems more an indication that one is lacking in true morality, that one needs something from the outside to control the otherwise unknown or unmanageable forces of the personality, that one distrusts nature, or finally that one is out of harmony with oneself and one's world. Naive dependency on external laws, rules, and restrictions could be thought of as conditions of the persona, the necessary and convenient mask a person wears to adjust to the demands of the external everyday world.

As such, obeying the law becomes a concession the individual makes to society that in effect cuts off certain aspects of the personality from being experienced and expressed. Favoring the persona over other aspects of the personality thins out a person's overall psychological presence. Such posturing in effect precludes the possibility of being in harmony (a joining together, agreement, concord) with oneself or the world, as too much of oneself and the world is missing. Jung comments,

> Every man is, in a certain sense, unconsciously a worse man when he is in society than when acting alone, for he is carried by society and to that extent is relieved of his individual responsibility. (CW 7, para. 240)

Psychologically speaking, then, such external laws rooted in society can block or inhibit the individual from exploring and relating to parts of the personality that must be taken into consideration if one is to be both authentically moral and psychologically whole. In an important sense, it seems one must know what it is like to break the law in order to be fully human.

Yet neither image strikes us as plausible: a world or culture in which there are no external laws or restrictions, or one where everyone goes about breaking the laws that do exist. Nor is Jung suggesting that we live our lives naively through either of those options. How then does the individual find that middle ground where he or she is both free and moral, both an individual and a part of society? One way of answering this question comes from an individual's confrontation with the inferior function and the shadow.

We have seen that confronting and acknowledging the inferior function and shadow is never as simple a matter as it sounds. The confrontation with the inferior function is not something a person generally seeks out. In fact, more often than not, it is the inferior function that comes after you. You bat it away; it comes back again . . . and again.

The parts of the personality associated with the inferior function and the shadow represent, to varying degrees, just those aspects of our individual and collective lives that the ego as well as all external laws and society seek to cage and tame. For reasons of stability and continuity, society does not want us playing around with our dark side; but, should these darker aspects of our personality continue to press upon consciousness, we too are most eager and willing to push them aside or away.

When given the opportunity to look at or claim our own dark side, we most commonly and conveniently project it onto something or someone else and then go on about our business as if nothing happened; persona strained, ego intact. *Projection*, then, is a pivotal psychological concept in any discussion of the inferior function as a moral problem, both on the individual and collective levels.

Earlier in our study, we developed the notion of polarity as it related to Jung's typology and overall psychology. We asserted then that the notion of polarity is a kind of metapsychological principle for Jung, pervasive and indisputable as a theoretical key to understanding many of his subsequent psychological insights. Methodologically speaking, the concept of projection acts in a similar manner. As the concept of polarity can help us understand the formal structure and dynamics of the psyche, the concept of projection brings us closer to the raw effects of an individual's psyche operating in the everyday world. Through the mechanism of projection, Jung explains, "everything that is unconscious in ourselves, we discover in our neighbor and we treat him accordingly" (CW 10, para. 131).

The term itself, which Jung adapted from Freud, means an unconscious, unperceived, and unintentional transfer of energy of subjective psychic elements onto an outer object. Jung also speaks of a "hook" that in everyday life serves as the object upon which the subjective psychic contents are projected (CW 8, para. 99).[1] What is important to realize here is that any psychic content can be projected onto any "fitting" object (person or thing). Therefore, in the vast variety of our projections, we have represented a vivid and panoramic display of psychic energy moving from the subjective unconscious to the objective world. Projections thus are the most immediate testimony of the unconscious operating in the world, as well as potentially one of the most damaging and dangerous characteristics of the human personality.

Let us first look at some "domestic" versions of projection that highlight the moral dimension involved in dealing with the inferior function. When a person projects aspects of his or her personality onto an object with which the ego is in accord (usually thought of as the "good" aspects of the personality), one may assume that the projection serves to bring the object closer to the person. This "intimacy" may eventually make for an increase in mutual understanding between the subject and object. Perhaps if the object were another person, projection in this sense may initiate what would become a friendship. Unconsciously, we often first see the virtue we believe to be in ourselves in just such a friend. Consciousness too is liable to rally to establish supportive "facts" and then go on to "test" the information gathered over time. With some work on both sides, perhaps the friendship will prove true and lasting.[2]

On the other hand, when a person projects aspects of his or her personality with which the ego is at odds (usually thought of as "bad" aspects of personality, or the inferior function), then projection may in fact serve to distance the object from the subject. The relationship between subject and object now becomes disdainful, repulsive, and even hateful. The object is so tinged with the negative aspects of the subject's unconscious that we may truly speak of it as the "enemy."

Unfortunately, the inferior function is often expressed through just such a projection. Jung comments, " . . . what we combat in the other person is usually our own inferior side" (CW 10, para. 131). The ego and consciousness, once infected with the inferior function in this sense, can bring ruin to the enemy, or (as easily) to oneself.

Even under the best of conditions, when consciousness is functioning normally for us, we are mutually vulnerable to the degree that we simply do not know the other person well enough. When we are not conscious of what is going on in regard to the other person, the unconscious is often around to fill the vacuum. Unfortunately, having to face the unfamiliar or the unknown often makes us mutually suspicious and fearful. The poet James Agee expresses this everyday sentiment in poignant terms:

> Almost any person, no matter how damaged and blinded, is infinitely more capable of intelligence and joy than he usually knows, and even if he had no reason to fear his own poisons, he has those in others to fear, to assume and take care for if he would not hurt both himself and that other person and the pure act itself beyond cure. (Agee, 1960, p. 590)

The various complications and ramifications of projection on the personal and interpersonal level, not to mention how such energy can become politicized, are truly inexhaustible.

Because the inferior function is so tied to the archaic and barbaric side of an individual's personality, we must realize that the inferior function, when it is at the heart of such projections, can actually be dangerous. Relating to the inferior function then becomes a problem of the first order because, as Jung comments, "barbarism must first be vanquished before freedom can be won," and freedom is won, as he states in *Psychological Types*, when "the basic root and driving forces of morality are felt by the individual as constituents of his own nature" (CW 6, para. 35).

To give us a better idea of how projection works, Jung draws our attention to what he calls "the archaic mind" (CW 10, paras. 127–47). He does not mean here to point disparagingly to the "barbarism" of primitive culture; "barbarism" as such would only be a criticism a modern culture could make upon itself. Instead, by studying primitive cultures and religion, Jung creates a fertile point of contact between modern civilization and our own inherited ancestral psychology, a connection Jung fully explores in dealing with the archetypes of the collective unconscious (CWs 5, 8, 9i, 9ii, 12–14). As the inferior function is the doorway to the unconscious, special attention is warranted to appreciate how this dimension in one's life can play itself out.

Drawing chiefly on the work of the anthropologist Levy-Bruhl, Jung posits that "projection results from the archaic *identity* of subject and object, but is properly so called only when the need to dissolve the identity with the object has already arisen" (CW 6, para. 783). The last point in this quote is especially significant. Unless or until it becomes necessary for a person to differentiate between the subject and object, projection will take place at a level which is often naively assumed to be the actual state of affairs; i.e., our projections are taken for reality as it must be. For the most part, projection in this sense gives us the illusion necessary to maintain our unconscious lives in the external world (*participation mystique*). The individual is accordingly eclipsed by the object which carries his or her (unconscious) projection.

This is what happens on a regular basis in primitive culture, though less so in modern culture, given the primacy of the individual and the evolution of modern ego-consciousness. In primitive culture, the individual is subordinate to the collective, whose myths and rituals represent how things must be. The myths carry the projections for the group; the rituals carry the power to mediate the projections. Everyone knows how and why they are what they are simply by being a part of the group.

Because primitive cultures project so much of the unconscious, one should not think that a certain amount of differentiation is not taking place; it is simply of another kind—a second-order differentiation in comparison to modern ego-consciousness. Primitive consciousness is based on the collective unconsciousness; modern consciousness, on the other hand, must work through the personal unconscious, the hidden life of the individual, to a deliberate awareness of the collective unconsciousness. In other words, modern consciousness is based on the individual and so must return there first when problems arise. Primitive man, unlike modern man, has no need of anything as personally indicting as an "inferior function" to draw his attention back to his collective psychology.

In other regards, the differentiation that takes place in external reality for primitive consciousness can be compared with the differentiation that takes place at the subjective level for modern consciousness. Both forms of consciousness are capable of great complexity, as modern psychology and primitive ritual amply demonstrate, but both cultures remain alien or strange to each other.

When projection does take place in modern culture, matters are actually more difficult to manage, due to the personal investment of energy which is absent in primitive cultures. In order to preserve our relationships with the objects of our projections and to maintain our personal continuity with the world as we have come to know it through our projections, we moderns often go to bizarre extremes to validate and stabilize our projections. This usually involves a special act of ego-consciousness itself (e.g., will to power), or at least the pretense of such. When consciousness becomes so entangled with projections, it becomes itself distorted or "false." In our modern culture this means we often act to justify our projections as being "logical," "normal," "right," "rational," etc., all the while refusing to recognize such attributes for what they are: the biases, defenses, and rationalizations of an often unsure and embattled ego. Projection of this kind amounts to a sophisticated form of narcissistic entitlement.

In more ancient times, projections were part of elaborate religious systems and mythologies that in turn would help the archaic mind mediate the forces of the unconscious at a level closer to the source of the projections themselves (namely, the archetypes). Strictly speaking, without individual consciousness to intervene and complicate matters at the subjective level, projections of the archaic mind could never be thought of as "false," or even pretentious. Because primitive man did not have the problem of consciousness to contend with as we moderns do—i.e., because he lived in a world where the individual was not an important issue—projections were for him simply and surely the truth. In Jung's formulation, "Primitive man is unpsychological. Psychic happenings take place outside him in an objective way. Even the things he dreams about are real to him; that is the only reason for paying attention to dreams" (CW 10, para. 128).

At least in ancient times (and now, wherever religion is still a factor in a person's life), religious systems and mythologies had the advantage of forcing people to take their projections seriously, as objective facts that must be attended to with care and deliberation. In return for this seriousness, a person was assured a rightful place in the cosmos and a meaningful existence. This is no mean achievement, as an age that is described by many as meaningless, boring, and alienating should readily realize. However, instead it takes something like our own sophisticated and biased culture to "see through" the cultures and mythologies of times past as nothing but a collection of naive superstitions or lies. We moderns of course do not consider ourselves so fortunately "deceived" as our ancient counterparts.

Unfortunately too, we have not yet been able to come up with much that can handle the forces of the unconscious as effectively as did the older religions and mythological systems of other times and places. The best many moderns can do is to claim technology for their religious system and mythology.[3]

In any case, the nature of projection now and then is the same: in projection, we are cleverly disguised to ourselves in the object of our attention. Historically speaking, the modern ego and consciousness are relatively late developments that ideally will mature to help the individual sort through the *participation mystique* that is the common characteristic of all projections. Jungian psychology may in fact be thought of as especially modern in this sense, as it is specifically meant to help us finish this task of consciousness (Edinger, 1984). Jung himself, speaking as a modern in the best sense of that term, comments:

> Our age wants to experience the psyche for itself. It wants original experience and not assumptions, though it is willing to make use of all existing assumptions as a means to this end, including those of recognized religions and the authentic sciences. (CW 10, para. 173)

Such is, in fact, the experiment of modern consciousness. However, as good as it sounds here, one must truly be concerned over the eventual price humankind will have to pay for its experiment. If one observes how easily and how often we moderns continue to project the negative aspects of our unconscious onto our neighbor, one is convinced neither of our general psychological understanding nor of our humanity. Indeed, there seems to be something especially hypocritical about a culture and society that so prides itself on its knowledge and accomplishments, and yet whose members still project so much of their dark side onto one another. Jung warns,

> The unconscious has an inimical or ruthless bearing towards consciousness only when the latter adopts a false or pretentious attitude. (CW 7, para. 346)

There are other considerations to take into account about our modern lives and the rise of modern consciousness. Because civilization and technology put so much destructive power at our disposal, and because as a rule we are so reluctant to own up to our negative projections, we are individually and collectively more at risk to ourselves and others than ever before in human history. To some this apprehension may seem unnecessarily apocalyptic. Since progress and technology are often believed to be the hallmarks of modern culture and capable of solving any problem, it is tantamount to heresy to question their authority and saving presence in our world.

But an eruption from the unconscious would testify to an inscrutable power that could easily dwarf any recent technological achievements. Again, Jung warns:

> Let man but accumulate sufficient energies of destruction and the devil within him will soon be unable to resist putting them to their fated use. (CW 10, para. 163)

Unfortunately, it is probably reasonable to say that those who identify too easily or glibly with our technologically sophisticated culture and who view projection as something only "the other guy does" are also those individuals whose devils grow most restless. Those too who look condescendingly at primitive cultures as nothing but a concatenation of mistakes, lies, and phantoms of the imagination, probably themselves deny having anything remotely resembling an "inferior function" or shadow. Just so, these individuals put themselves (and everyone around them) at greater risk.

The volatile situation in the modern world should put us all on guard about how we deal with our respective inferior functions, especially those who are capable of abusing the power of technology as a destructive vehicle of inferior expression: I mean here the scientists and the politicians who are in leadership roles in their respective professions. The mythology that modernity presents to us, a mythology that says among other things that we do not need mythology, is infinitely more destructive than what any ancient or primitive culture would have been capable of enacting. We all in this sense need to be psychologists or students of the psyche.

It is becoming increasingly obvious that our moral education and sense of individual responsibility have not kept up with our technological progress as a culture; and increasingly fewer of us have the mediating influences of organized religion to help us sort through our projections in any meaningful way. This makes us all especially vulnerable should the unconscious erupt in a negative form. Combine this situation with the amount of technological power at our disposal and one can understand the anxiety that seems to be so much a part of modern life. In the depths of the modern psyche is the abject fear that what we have created in our own image has turned against us, has gone out of control, has become destructively "other."

We now have no alternative but to take the battle literally to heart, or risk acting out the battle in a world we profess to know so well. This is precisely what Jung is calling our attention to in his evocations of the inferior function as a moral issue. "The upheaval of the world and the upheaval of our consciousness are one and the same" (CW 10, para. 177), he tells us soberly. If we persist in being blind to the forces of the unconscious in our individual and collective lives and remain sadly naive about the uses and abuses of our science and technology, catastrophe certainly awaits us. It would be tragic indeed if we had to learn this lesson at the expense of the very culture we so extol.

Notes

1. Marie-Louise von Franz (1985) has provided an exhaustive and insightful treatment of this topic in her book *Projection and Recollection in Jungian Psychology*. In the Foreword she comments, "If nothing but epistemological considerations were involved [in looking at problems associated with projection], perhaps we could let the matter drop; but the phenomenon of projection is also an eminently moral and practical problem . . . "

2. Of that special friendship we call marriage, I am unable to confirm Jung and von Franz's conclusion that people tend to marry their typological opposites in order to complement their own types (see CW 17, paras. 324–345, and von Franz, 1984, p. 4). Their rationale is that individuals marry through an unconscious motivation, to insure that their respective inferior parts would be taken care of by the partner. In this sense, a strongly introverted thinking type would seek out an extraverted feeling type to become "whole," each using the marriage relationship to avoid owning up to and integrating the inferior part of his or her personality. The fact that such marriages did *not* go smoothly is what interested Jung.

Marriage today is a different kind of refuge. I would advance the hypothesis that opposite types are indeed still unconsciously attracted to one another, but usually in the context of short-term extramarital relationships. As a consequence, for many couples marriage is not the hotbed of individuation it may once have been.

For various reasons, individuals are *consciously* looking for something psychologically safe in a marriage partner, which is latter compensated for, at the unconscious level, through a "dangerous (exciting, romantic) affair." With respect to marriage, desire has given way to the "sharing" of a life together; the security of mutual similarity is winning out over exasperation at the prospect of having to work out "irreconcilable differences."

3. It is no longer unusual to see back-page articles in the newspaper such as the one by Lee Siegel (Associated Press, August 28, 1988), entitled "Atom Smasher's Glitches Block View of God's Mind":

> LOS ANGELES—Physicists wanting to "understand what's in the mind of God" are frustrated by glitches in a new $115 million atom smasher that someday may yield secrets about the makeup of matter and the birth of the universe.

May we presume that the physicists who find this information know how to handle their newly acquired knowledge?

V

Contexts and Contacts

The psyche is a whole in which everything is connected with everything else.

(CW 16, para. 462)

BEFORE WE GO ON to put Jungian typology in the context of Jung's general psychological model, it will be helpful to reverse field and see how typology was used by Jung as a context for developing his own *Weltanschauung*. One's philosophy of life or worldview and one's consciousness are intimately tied together. Jung went so far in *Psychological Types* as to say that "consciousness is always in the nature of a *Weltanschauung*, if it is not explicitly a religion. It is this that makes the type problem so important" (CW 6, para. 911).

Jung, then, views typology, his "psychology of consciousness," not only as a way to see how an individual packages and relates to the inner and outer worlds, but also as key to understanding a person's worldview. So true and useful is this statement that we want to see how it applies to Jung himself.

Obviously, as the "inventor" of typology, we may suspect that Jung had an edge in putting together his own worldview. In a sense, typology gave him an Archimedian point from which to build his position. In addition to using typology for self-knowledge, and sorting through and understanding the similarities and differences between individuals in a clinical setting, Jung could use his typological insights to position himself in the culture of his time so as to be able to advance a critique of modern consciousness in the West as part of his own *Weltanschauung.*

To make some sense how Jung did this, some background is needed as to the importance of philosophy itself in Jung's life, as well as some understanding of the differences between psychology and philosophy for Jung.

Jung was by no means trained as a philosopher. However, the influence of Kant, Schopenhauer, Burckhardt, and Nietzsche are very conspicuous in his works. During an interview in which he was recounting his initial excitement about going into the then new and risky field of psychiatry, Jung stated:

> In my last semester I was preparing for my final exam and I had to know something about psychiatry, so I took up Krafft-Ebing's textbook on psychiatry. I read first the introduction . . . and then it happened. Then it happened. I thought, this is it, this is the confluence of medicine and philosophy! This is what I have been looking for! (Hull and McGuire, 1977, p. 209)

Jung's early commitment to philosophy (see, for example, *The Zofingia Lectures,* 1896–1899) gave him an amazing facility for using philosophical concepts to describe and explain psychological facts as he saw them. A psychological fact was anything relating to the psyche, i.e., anything that was a part of the interrelations between consciousness and the unconscious. As such, psychological facts did not need to stand the test of philosophical, or worse, metaphysical, truth. Rather, psychological facts had to be taken first and most importantly as anything coming from the psyche, which theoretically meant that virtually anything was grist for the psychologist's mill.

However, at the time Jung began his work, psychology had not yet evolved a discourse in which it could maneuver the full variety or potential of "psychological facts" that were in Jung's own time already on the record, e.g., mythologies, fairy tales, dreams, the nonsensical utterances of schizophrenics, etc.

Besides, psychology had the added problem that the object of its science, the object of its *logos*, was the psyche itself. This meant that the psyche of the psychologist was always being implicated in any psychological statements. This subjective element compounded the problem of doing research by placing the psychologist in a field from which it was very difficult to claim sufficient "detachment" to warrant respect from the otherwise "hard" sciences. Jung also never tired of remarking that because of the subjective element in psychology, everyone who ventured into the field would claim to be an "expert."

Jung never hid this subjective element, of which we will have much more to say shortly, from himself or those interested in his work. He even went so far as to say that all psychological models were first of all the "subjective confessions" of those who came up with them. This candor on Jung's part is refreshing. He unashamedly acknowledges his own subjectivity in his work, which paradoxically allows him to account for his biases more honestly, and so to achieve a relatively greater degree of "objectivity" than may otherwise have been possible. People attracted to Jungian psychology invariably appreciate this aspect of Jung's approach. As was mentioned earlier, the laboratory that Jungian psychology first takes one to is oneself.

However, one cannot remain *utterly* subjective, nor is life meant to be lived in a laboratory. Jung's partial solution to having to deal with the subjective element in psychology was to insist that analysts themselves be analyzed. The reasoning behind this standard is that one must get to know the insides of one's own laboratory sufficiently well and with some relative "objectivity" before poking around in others'. This was hardly a complete or final solution to the problem, but it seemed a step in the right direction. The statement Jung was making by requiring that analysts themselves be analyzed was a significant concession to the overwhelming power and *value* of the subjective element in doing psychological work with others.

For practical purposes right now, the problem of inter-

preting psychological facts from a subjective perspective may
be best summed up as follows:

> Upon one's own philosophy, conscious or unconscious,
> depends one's ultimate interpretation of the facts. There-
> fore, it is wise to be as clear as possible about one's own
> subjective principles. (quoted in Jacobi, 1953, pp. 112–113)

Ultimately, for Jung, then, psychology could use philosophical concepts provided it did so consciously and responsibly; philosophy itself was considered a means to become
"as clear as possible about one's own subjective principles."
The seventy-eight pages of "definitions" that are included in
Psychological Types represent one way in which Jung "made
clear" his "subjective principles." He makes the effort in
other ways in other of his books.

While some philosophers believe Jung is profligate in his
use of terms such as "subject," "object," "abstract," "concrete," "rational," "irrational," "perception," "appercep-
tion," "symbol," "semiotic," "soul," "idea," "concept,"
indeed "consciousness" and "the unconscious," Jung himself
does take great pains to be as clear as he can with philosophical concepts, given his psychological motivations. The problem that Jung had with philosophy per se was that it appeared
to him too "systematic" a discipline, meaning too confining
or too closed in on itself, to do the psyche justice. Philosophers would be less bothered by Jung if they realized that philosophy for him was a kind of "greenhouse for consciousness" rather than a full-blown garden, as many philosophical
systems often are.

To move now into the meaning and place of Jung's
Weltanschauung, we must go further with our understanding
of the meaning of "subjectivity" for Jung, as this notion goes
to the heart of Jung's critique of Western consciousness.

Jung's understanding of subjectivity is not what the word
may first suggest to many Westerners, namely to be lost in
the fumes of a passionless, spiritless, or self-indulgent introspection. Jung himself had a keen sense of history and an
excellent ability to decipher the grand psychological effects
of continuity and change, cause and effect, upon the individual. Subjectivity, he knew, did not remove one from history

or from the spirit of the times. Of the importance of a person's historical-cultural circumstances, Jung tells us:

> Every individual problem is somehow connected to the problem of the ages, so that practically every subjective difficulty has to be viewed from the standpoint of the human situation as whole. (CW 10, para. 323)

One of the problems of the ages for Jung was the devaluation of subjectivity itself. This is why the issue can likewise be considered part of Jung's own *Weltanschauung.* The problem may be sorted through as follows:

Ever since the seventeenth century, consciousness in the West has had to contend with the problem of the individual separated from the world by his or her own mind. As an idea, Descartes' celebrated and notorious *cogito ergo sum* (I think, therefore I am) has become the symbol for this kind of cleavage between subject and object. In the case of the *cogito,* "being" is first taken as a consequence of "thinking."

Typologically speaking, this means that the subjective "I" is separated from the object and defined reductively by one of the four functions. Implicit in the formulation is the devaluation of the subject apart from its ability to think. Or, conversely, the "I" is elevated in proportion to its ability to think. The rational "thinking" function is therefore dignified as superior to the world from which it arose and held out as the supreme function and asset of man, something to aspire to, something that confers "status" and power.

For Jung, the common result of such a point of view translates into typological behavior representing an exaggerated thinking function that supports the ego, but which in a profound sense is disconnected from the ego's true source of being in its own subjectivity and with the world.

As one might suspect, science has been the chief beneficiary of Cartesian thinking. Because of the productive illusion of the intellect acting apart from its subjectivity in an almost disembodied manner, it became increasingly easy for science to view rational thinking itself as an autonomous and highly regarded power, a power indeed that has proven itself in history to be godlike. With great confidence, science has thus been able to go "forward" seemingly unimpeded by any psychological, i.e., subjective, considerations. All disciplines, including psychology, feel even now that to be taken seriously they must be more and more like science in this rationalistic sense.

As one might imagine, this split in the Western psyche and the overemphasis on the rational mind at the expense of everything else has been nothing short of disastrous for individuals outside the scientific elite. It is of course no coincidence that our ability to split the atom, i.e., our ability to destroy ourselves, is now an ever-present danger that has penetrated into the dream life of young school-age children. Perhaps what is most irksome here is that the scientific elite responsible for making the destructive abilities of the psyche such a keen reality continues to have its own intellect for company and enjoys a dominant position in our culture. Meanwhile, those who believe themselves to be typologically miscast in this drama (feeling- and sensing-types especially), or those who are typologically too immature to handle the "split" (those growing up), become increasingly frightened and feel increasingly "out of touch" with their world.

In this regard, Jung's work then and now can be viewed typologically as compensatory to an age which values the rational thinking function at the expense of the other three functions. Jung's typology allowed him to see how lopsided Western culture had become and gave him the necessary motivation to consciously provide a psychology that could reveal such an imbalance as well as suggest means for correcting it. But there is more.

Jung viewed the devaluation of the subject in Western consciousness just as critically as he viewed the idolatry of the rational thinking function, if not more so. This comes out most clearly in the typological comparisons he makes between Eastern and Western consciousness. In addition to being a major characteristic of Western consciousness, the kind of subject-object split that we have been talking about is also the major historical and psychological difference between Western and Eastern consciousness, a difference which Jung claims cannot be overlooked.

Eastern consciousness is in fact made up first of all of "the subjective factor," or what Jung refers to as a relation to "the eternal patterns of psychic functioning" (CW 11, para.

778). "The subjective factor" in this sense is the very thing Western consciousness characteristically neglects; it is everything unknown to the rational and objective intellect which has disembodied itself and separated from the world.

In *Psychological Types*, Jung is clearly trying to rehabilitate "the subjective factor" for Western consciousness (CW 6, paras. 645–649). He calls it "a co-determinant of the world we live in, a factor that can on no account be left out of our calculations . . . the subjective factor is as ineluctable a datum as the extent of the sea and the radius of the earth" (CW 6, para. 622).

Why are there such large differences between Eastern and Western consciousness? Why does the West so neglect "the subjective factor"? Taking the risk of overextending the categories of extraversion and introversion, Jung understands Eastern consciousness as orienting itself through centuries of introversion (showing a preference for the subject and the experience of relating to the "eternal patterns of psychic functioning"); Western consciousness is viewed as orienting itself primarily and most recently through extraversion (showing a preference for the object) (see especially CW 11, paras. 759–787). This creates the respective cultural bias of each culture. Jung's *Weltanschauung* is here made clear through the application of his typology.

These larger cultural contexts in which we find Jung applying his typological terminology serve as the beginnings of a cultural hermeneutics that can help us better understand and appreciate cultural diversity. With this in mind, one could possibly find a particular introvert from the United States who would seem to be a glowing extravert in the East, so telling are the psychological differences between the two cultures.

Along these same lines, some Westerners who fancy themselves introverts often allow themselves to believe that they have an automatic familiarity or privileged relationship to the subjective or interior life. This is certainly not the case. Introversion is not subjectivity or even introspection; introversion is an attitude preference or "turning toward" the subjective or interior life. To look at and to relate to the unconscious wherever and however it presents itself is a whole other ball game, as any introvert in analysis would tell you. In this sense, the stereotype of the "profound" introvert is as misleading as the stereotype of the "superficial" extravert.

Because the introverted Eastern consciousness takes "the subjective factor" as a natural starting point, it is not in need of a psychology or typology of the kind which Jung is advocating. However, in the West, which is so intently object-oriented and rational, Jung's emphasis on "the subjective factor" becomes an important contribution to the problem of consciousness characteristic of both Jung's and our own age. Of course, the East is not quite the same as when Jung was making his typological observations (Jung is referring to a premodern or pre-"Westernized" East). But Jung's description of Western consciousness as bound up with the object is probably even more true today than when he was writing, and this notwithstanding the apparent influx of Eastern thinking into the West, or the "New Age."

The rehabilitation of "the subjective factor" is ultimately the aspect of Jung's work that still confuses people the most. It is here that Jung is criticized as being too Eastern, too mystical, not scientific, narcissistic, or, worst of all, solipsistic. One should not think that Jung is going "East" for his psychology, or that by accenting "the subjective factor" in his own work he is claiming a convenient tentativeness about his findings, or that his psychology is simply and comfortably for himself. Rather, Jung's emphasis on "the subjective factor" reflects his belief that the legitimate beginning for any authentic (Western) psychology is with the problems and conflicts of one's own psyche in the day and age one finds oneself living. One cannot easily jump over oneself, or one's place in history.

Jung, aware of his own vulnerabilities to his Western public, always insisted on being taken seriously as a Western empiricist, which had the effect of landing him squarely in the world Westerners all share. Typology was an excellent tool to substantiate that claim and he used it wisely to base his own convictions. In regard to Jung's alleged mysticism, as Aniela Jaffé has commented, Jung was, of all things and despite all evidence to the contrary, "anxious to be understood" (1971, p. 127). Few mystics are as anxious, or, I might add, as productive.

As Jung's psychology is not meant for the East, the Eastern way of thinking is not meant for the West. The emphasis on subjectivity in Jung's thinking does not mean that he believes Western consciousness should simply imitate the external forms of Eastern consciousness. Because of the East's intimate and historical awareness of "the subjective factor" as part of the psyche, Jung feels that Eastern consciousness has much to teach us about our own individual and collective unconscious. But it cannot take us around our own cultural-historical conditioning.

This may be phrased another way: the Western ego, the source of so many of our problems, cannot be abandoned in the exploration of the unconscious. Jung understands the ego to be the carrier or vehicle of consciousness (CW 6, para. 706), and as such it is an important and necessary achievement that Westerners should not forsake, or pretend is not there. Staying faithful to ego-consciousness as a problem is Jung's way of staying faithful to his Western roots. Jung comments:

> To us, consciousness is inconceivable without an ego; it is equated with the relation of contents to an ego. If there is no ego there is nobody to be conscious of anything. The ego is therefore indispensable to the conscious process. The Eastern mind, however, has no difficulty in conceiving of a consciousness without ego. (CW 11, para. 774)

Both the stance which Jung takes against the overvaluation of the thinking function and his revaluation of the importance of the subjective (or interior, unconscious) life of the individual make up a critical part of Jung's own *Weltanschauung*. In both instances, typology is used to formulate and substantiate his critique of modern Western consciousness, within a point of view that is characteristic of Western consciousness itself. Only then does Jung find Western consciousness in a very precarious position in regard to the unconscious. He comments:

> In the West, the conscious standpoint arbitrarily decides against the unconscious, since anything coming from inside suffers from the prejudice of being regarded as inferior or somehow wrong. (CW 11, para. 780)

And here we have our turning point, what will connect us to Jung's depth psychology. The way into the unconscious for

Westerners, to an experience of "the subjective factor," is often only through the painful and personal experience of dealing with the devalued and inferior side of one's psyche. This is not the way of the East.

Typology, through the inferior function, is the facet of Jungian psychology that deals directly with ego-consciousness as a problem. It would seem Jung is saying that it is wise to account for the various patterns of ego-consciousness *before* one embarks on a "study" of the patterns of the unconscious, "the subjective factor" itself. The experience that comes when the inferior function takes the ego into the unconscious and shows it firsthand that the patterns it has based itself on are in turn based on something else—something more powerful, more disturbing, even more "objective" than anything it has accustomed itself to knowing—is what finally allows Jung's larger psychological model to make sense.

A psychological typology which takes the individual ego in the everyday world as its starting point can be especially helpful in correcting the Western bias against the unconscious and its idolatry of the thinking function. With its realization of four psychological functions rather than just one (e.g., thinking), and two attitudes rather than just one (e.g., extraversion), differences are better recognized and understanding is broadened and enhanced. Combine this with the dynamic principle of polarity at the heart of Jung's typological model and one can see how an understanding of typology would help an individual to do what it did for Jung, namely, to acknowledge the richness of the "subjective factor" as part of legitimate psychological work and to develop and maneuver creatively within one's own *Weltanschauung.*

We are now ready to shift ground and put typology in the context of Jung's general psychology.

The Inferior Function, Jungian Psychology, and the Archetypal Self

If we were to diagram Jung's typology without the individual's experience of the inferior function as a factor to be taken into consideration, the diagram could look like this:

Typology from the Perspective of Ego-Consciousness

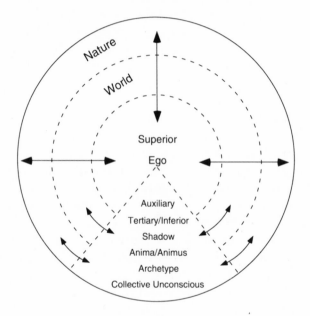

In our diagram, ego-consciousness is positioned in the center of both the world and nature. It is the prerogative and need of ego-consciousness to set things up on such terms. Indeed, by a process of marking off and developing one's psychological identity, the person learns to handle the world as it impinges on an emerging and fragile consciousness. One's life would be totally unmanageable should such development not take place.

The arrows moving through all three concentric circles signify psychic activity in and out of the world, nature, and consciousness. But fundamentally it is because the ego is the "fixed" point, the "hub" of reality as the person may come to know it, that the personality can withstand being over-whelmed by outside forces larger than itself. One's psycho-logical type is, of course, prominent in the inner circle, the dominant/superior and auxiliary functions clearly being illustrated in ego-consciousness.

Nonetheless, the inner circle of ego-consciousness is being penetrated by a wedge from the unconscious. The wedge represents different aspects of the unconscious as one would find them described in Jung's general psychology. On the periphery of consciousness are the tertiary and inferior functions, followed by the *shadow*, the *anima/animus*, and other of the archetypes. Finally, the collective unconscious in its most archaic, instinctual, or animalistic form is at the bottom of the wedge. The arrows at this bottom layer of the wedge represent activity between the collective unconscious and nature. For the most part, consciousness would relate to these strange contents from the collective unconscious in a naive fashion, through projection.

The dotted lines separating everything inside the larger cir-cle signify the fluid nature of what is taking place in the psy-che. Nature flows easily into and out of the collective uncon-scious, and moves slowly up the pyramid through the archetypes to consciousness. The archetypes represent nature in image form as it relates to the individual. Jung often referred to the archetypes as "the self-portraits of the instincts."

From birth on, consciousness, arising out of the uncon-scious, works to center itself and in turn moves out to con-quer the world and nature. One could imagine a state of inflated ego-consciousness as the inner circle grows to the point where it finally is identical with the world and nature, being puffed up along the way with the mysterious contents and power of the unconscious itself.

Giving the diagram a typological interpretation, we would say that the chief purpose of the ego would be to devel-op and maintain the person's successful psychological type. That is, the individual must differentiate certain aspects of the personality that it can rely on to handle problems of the world and nature. Typologically speaking, this means devel-oping one's preferences for either introversion or extraver-sion, sensation or intuition, thinking or feeling. The preferences that are not selected by consciousness drop into the wedge, into the unconscious, where they are contaminated by contents from the unconscious.

When an individual's consciousness becomes restrictive or complacent, i.e., when personality development is too one-sided or, in the diagram, should the inner circle become rigid and closed off, the overall functioning of the personality becomes negatively affected; the balance and flow of psychic energy are upset. The elements of the personality which have been neglected go into conflict with ego-consciousness. Once the inferior functions have begun to make themselves felt, and the problem of opposites is constellated, the entire unconscious itself can take its toll on the personality.

A decisive experience with the inferior function in effect opens up ego-consciousness to the reality of the psyche. This is usually in negative form because the unconscious has to force itself on consciousness. Looking at the wedge, one can get the sense of the unconscious having to push itself up and into consciousness. Moreover, the opening into conscious-ness gets bigger as one works one's way down the wedge, making consciousness itself more and more vulnerable from the psychic energy underneath. One can also recall here the "door" metaphor which both Jung and von Franz use to sig-nify the opening through which the unconscious makes its presence felt on the conscious personality.

When the inferior function filters into the personality, it is possible for ego-consciousness to gradually fill up with neg-ative contents from the unconscious. The archetypes of the unconscious then present a horrendous problem to the ego, whose main problem now becomes trying to handle the over-flow of energy from "below."

The archetypes shown in the diagram are those which, according to Jung, are "most clearly characterized from the empirical point of view." That is, they are the archetypes "which have the most frequent and disturbing influence on the ego. These are the *shadow*, the *anima*, and the *animus*" (CW 9ii, para. 13). The diagram also shows that other arche-types exist in the unconscious and may be more difficult to characterize.

When the ego has to contend with the unconscious, it will either trench in and resist, identify with contents from the unconscious, project the unconscious contents out to the world, or try to relate to the unconscious on fitting terms. Most often, the individual will try all four clumsily or in desperation. However, as we have seen, the first three courses court disaster. Only the last course is truly a conscious and moral option.

Once one turns to the unconscious to relate to it, certain transformations can take place. Clearly, a person who has had a decisive experience with the inferior function in this manner and turns to the despised parts of his or her personality in the proper spirit is not the same as before the experience. One's sense of self changes as well as the way one experiences the world.

The ego is in effect knocked out of center, the individual thrown off balance; the world and nature change their meanings and parameters; even one's notion of time changes. This all comes from a true experience of the unconscious, which the inferior function has the power to mediate or put into effect. Jung comments:

> . . . I regard the loss of balance as purposive, since it replaces a defective consciousness by the automatic and instinctive activity of the unconscious, which is aiming all the time at the creation of a new balance and will moreover achieve this aim, provided the conscious mind is capable of assimilating the contents produced by the unconscious, i.e., of understanding and digesting them. (CW 7, para. 253)

In effect, Jung is saying that when ego-consciousness defined by a particular psychological type proves to be "defective," i.e., one-sided or rigid, the unconscious will bring the individual back into balance. This, however, usually involves an encounter with the inferior function, that part of the personality through which the unconscious most forcefully acts. The inferior function is seen negatively as the source of the "loss of balance" for the ego, but positively and purposely as something whose source exists outside the ego itself.

Once this negativity is seen as part of the purposeful movement of the psyche, one's attitude changes in regard to the inferior function as well. No one can say why or how or when this happens, but experientially we know that it does.

This is why it is important to be attentive to the unconscious when one is facing the inferior function. Through the inferior function comes not only one's misery and suffering, but also, as von Franz has said, the archetype of the Self.

Provided that the ego, the carrier of consciousness, is not swallowed or destroyed by the affront from the unconscious, the individual now has the opportunity of assimilating the neglected and troublesome parts of the personality and regaining a new perspective, a new balance for itself. With the increase in consciousness of those neglected parts of the personality, additional psychic energy is also released and the experience of the Self becomes a greater possibility.

In the passage above, Jung points to the self-regulatory aspect of the psyche as a purposeful act. To achieve a new balance implies something other than sheer opposition; it indicates meaningful movement of the psyche to re-order itself according to its own principles or laws—a *telos* is implied.

When consciousness and the unconscious work in a complementary relationship with one another, i.e., when one is following and cooperating with one's own inner laws and destiny, Jung refers to the regulating principle and the totality of the psyche itself as the experience of the archetypal Self. The Self, Jung explains,

> is a quantity that is supraordinate to the conscious ego. It embraces not only the conscious but also the unconscious psyche, and is therefore, so to speak, a personality which we *also* are. (CW 7, para. 274)

The individuation process is a process of psychological development that fulfills the qualities and requirements of the Self. It is the person consciously becoming this "other" personality.

However, there is a paradox. If the Self contains consciousness and the unconscious, consciousness will never be able to fully assimilate the Self, will never be able to be fully "other." This would in effect mean that consciousness could contain the unconscious, a state of being which could qualify oneself for deification.

Here is the rub: the unconscious needs consciousness to become aware of it, and the archetypal Self is what takes each person his or her own way along this journey. While it is the nature of the Self to have to realize itself in consciousness, this is a task that theoretically cannot be completed without the evolution of a new form of consciousness to incarnate the paradox. Jung comments:

> There is little hope of our ever being able to reach even approximate consciousness of the self, since however much we make conscious there will always exist an indeterminate and indeterminable amount of unconscious material which belongs to the totality of the self. (CW 7, para. 274)

Because of this paradoxical quality of the Self, it has been described as "smaller than small, and greater than great" (CW 6, para. 329): that is, smaller than the ego itself, but without compass. Or, to use a medieval metaphor for God, the Self is "a circle whose circumference is nowhere and whose center is everywhere."

Both metaphors as such often translate into an experience in which the individual feels that he or she is in effect in communion with God, "centered" in the inner and outer worlds all at once. The split between subject and object, thinking and feeling, consciousness and the unconscious, gives way to relation. The Self in this way becomes the great reconciler of opposites as well.

Jung goes into fine detail in many of his works on such aspects of this extremely difficult archetype to understand (see CW 9ii, especially paras. 347–421, and CW 14). However, we will turn again to the poets who are especially adept at conveying what Jung is approaching from a more analytical point of view. Rilke's poem "A Walk" beautifully expresses the feeling of experiencing the Self:

> My eyes already touch the sunny hill,
> going far ahead of the road I have begun.
> So we are grasped by what we cannot grasp.
> It has its inner light, even from a distance
> And changes us, even if we do not reach it,
>   into something else,
> which, hardly sensing it, we already are;
> A gesture waves us on answering our own wave
> But what we feel is the wind in our faces.

The play between ego and Self in this poem is truly startling. First, the experience occurs in something as simple as "A Walk"—not even "*The* Walk." Throughout the poem there is the sense of an instantaneous communion with reality, an appreciation of being both apart and a part, yet identical with and contained in the whole. There is also the sense that the ego is being taken by the Self, not that it has contrived or forced the experience, but that it is being led. The change which is worked on the ego takes place even if the ego does not reach the Self. The change takes place in the *relationship* between the ego and the Self, in the experiencing of this numinous moment. The "destiny" of the walk is the moment of consciousness, which in turn is "the wind in our faces."

Our friend Kabir, with his poem "The Fish in the Sea Is Not Thirsty," gives us another angle on the experience of the Self:

> Inside this clay jug there are
> canyons and pine mountains, and
> the maker of canyons and pine mountains!
>
> All seven oceans are inside
> and hundreds of millions of stars.
> The acid that tests gold is there,
> And the one who judges jewels
> And the music from the strings no one touches,
> and the source of all water.
>
> If you want truth, I will tell you the truth:
> Friend, listen: The God whom I love is inside.

Again, one is struck by the simplicity of a clay jug as a vessel or container for the universe itself. This time Kabir's vision takes him inside, to the limitless being whom he calls God. The tone of this poem actually has a sting to it. Kabir is making a response to someone, someone to whom his voice carries a strong level of conviction. Could he be talking to his own ego? Again, we have a metaphor for the Self in relation.

Both poems are very delicate, in the sense that one does not want to overinterpret them. Perhaps this is also a sign of their strength. In any case, the decisive step that is taken through the poems is that something qualitatively different from one's own ego, something beyond the conscious side of one's own psychological type, has now made its presence decisively felt. Because the ego itself is involved in the experience, i.e., the experience has been brought to consciousness and consciousness has "digested" it, the ego now feels connected to the Self, even defined by it.

There is, of course, a big presumption behind all of this: that the ego can and will turn to the unconscious in its time of suffering and relate to it honestly. But it is nothing less than this connection that Jung's psychology points out and builds on.

The concept of the Self is as important to Jungian psychology as it is to the development of the individual personality. Jung's typology, in focusing on how the conscious personality shapes and patterns itself, gives us a way to comprehend the ego. Jung's depth psychology, in focusing on the function of the Self in the personality, allows us to see the connection between the ego and the Self, between consciousness and the unconscious.

Not surprisingly, Jung tells us that how we solve our moral problems is the compelling factor in becoming who we must become. Typologically speaking, the inferior function is a moral issue that keeps the individuation process going. Jung comments:

> In the last resort it is a man's moral qualities which force him, either through direct recognition of the need or indirectly through a painful neurosis, to assimilate his unconscious self and to keep himself fully conscious. (CW 7, para. 218)

To summarize so far: in Jung's general psychology, the psyche, made up of consciousness and the unconscious, reflects and includes our particular empirical reality. As we participate in both consciousness and the unconscious, theoretically we can come to understand one and the other. However, the archetype of the Self, representing the totality of the relationship between consciousness and the unconscious, can never be completely known. The part can never contain the whole—except as paradox or metaphor (poetry!) in consciousness.

Once one has had a taste of the Self, even a negative one, as through an encounter with the inferior function, one cannot go back to "business as usual." In the case of a severe confrontation with the inferior function, the ego has been too severely displaced or broken down in favor of something "other," something it knows all too well but only by its effects and occasionally through images and dreams. In less extreme cases, intimations of the Self become compelling instances in one's life that can no longer be ignored.

Given this experience, to go on fighting the world from a perspective of ego-centrism or through one's projections would be to consign oneself to flailing away in shallow waters until one tires out and drowns. In such cases, the Self would clamor back, "if one is to drown, then let it be in my depths."

The diagram on page 128 illustrates the change and development that take place in the overall personality once one has been able to relate to the unconscious and make the experience of the Self a reality. The diagram also puts Jungian typology in the larger context of Jungian psychology.

In the diagram, one can best understand the dynamics between typology and Jungian psychology by looking at the relationship between the ego and the Self. As consciousness can be described typologically, the unconscious can be described archetypally. And, as the ego is the center of consciousness, Jung posits the archetypal Self as the center of the psyche as a whole.

The ego and the Self are connected at center points in a manner of relationship which is called the ego-Self axis (Edinger, 1972, pp. 3–8). Jung speaks of the goal of individuation as "sensing the self as something irrational, as an indefinable existent, to which the ego is neither opposed nor subjected, but merely attached, and about which it revolves very much as the earth revolves around the sun . . . " (CW 7, para. 405).

The smaller circle circulating around the larger one signifies a transformed consciousness simultaneously moving through the outer world and the unconscious—the ego moving around the Self.

As the center and carrier of consciousness, the ego is still

Typology from the Perspective of the Archetypal Self

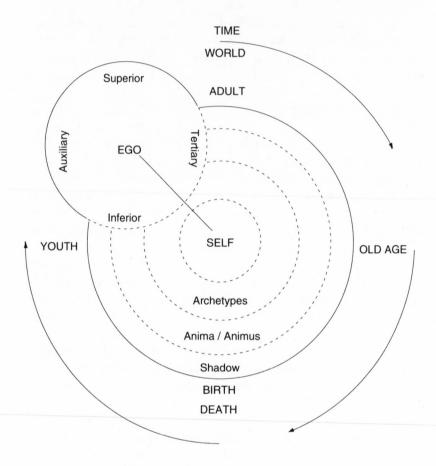

described by the four functions. Two functions are shown as developed and existing exclusively for the benefit of the ego's relationship to the world. The other two functions partake of the larger circle, the unconscious, and overlap with the archetypes. In this diagram, the inferior function(s) are the first part of the personality which consciousness discovers en route to sorting out what Jung calls "the dominants of the unconscious," i.e., the archetypes.

As consciousness differentiates its tertiary and inferior functions, the shadow reveals itself. After relating to and assimilating contents from the shadow, the archetypes of the anima or animus will make themselves felt, and so on.[1] As one moves through archetypal images, one is taking in more and more of the dark and unknown parts of one's personality. Each archetype in this regard has a shadow aspect to it.

The diagram also illustrates consciousness in proximity to the psyche's archetypal core. One suspects that one can get even closer to the archetypal Self than is implied by the diagram, but in any case consciousness will never contain it or claim it in its totality. In fact, the intimation of the presence of the Self through symbols and images is the most that we could theoretically point to. But, as in all cases of relating to contents of the unconscious, the experience is what counts.

To put the diagram into motion, one could imagine living one's life moving around and through the larger circle and through the world. If energy is withdrawn from the ego's attachment to the world, the unconscious benefits. But if too much energy is withdrawn from the world or too much energy devoted to it, the unconscious itself becomes too active and overwhelms the ego. This is what can happen when the ego breaks down in the face of a serious confrontation with the inferior function. The smaller circle, consciousness, is then unwillingly pulled into the larger circle, the unconscious, and the ego fights for dear life.

Therapeutically speaking, because of its relationship with consciousness the ego must not fall completely into the unconscious. Neither is it in the ego's own interest to "go after" the unconscious or to seek to conquer the Self. In such cases, the dark side of the Self takes over the ego, an experience akin to meeting one's inferior function a hundredfold. Jung comments, "It must be reckoned a psychic catastrophe when the *ego is assimilated by the self*" (CW 9ii, para. 45. Italics in original).

This frightening possibility takes us back to typology proper, to looking at typology with a new and qualified respect as pointing to the development of one's conscious psychological type. To view typology as "the beginning and end of the individuation process," in Meier's cropped phrase, is now not only a possibility but a necessity as well. We must see ourselves both as ego and Self if we are to move through the unconscious in a meaningful way. Jung finally tells us:

> It is of the greatest importance that the ego should be
> anchored in the world of consciousness and that conscious-
> ness should be reinforced by a very precise adaptation. For
> this, certain virtues like attention, conscientiousness,
> patience, etc., are of great value on the moral side. Just as
> accurate observation of the symptomatology of the uncon-
> scious and objective self-criticism are valuable on the intel-
> lectual side. (CW 9ii, para. 46)

We may conclude with a speculation that comes from
staring at this diagram too long. One suspects that as consciousness passes the midpoint of its journey around the
large circle, it begins to fall into the large circle on its own,
part of the inexorable laws of the Self acting on the ego to
bring it "home." But if one's conscious connection to the Self
is strong, the process of going back into the large circle need
not take place against one's will. When timed properly, it
could be most enlightening. In this way, one may even
"choose" one's death, having practiced at it so much in the
course of a life. That is, at the right time one may willingly
and knowingly return consciousness to the psyche that was
the cradle of its birth. While psychosis is often experienced as
a kind of dying or death, death itself need not be a psychotic
experience.

The Transcendent Function

> Everything good is costly, and the development of personal-
> ity is one of the most costly of all things. It is a matter of
> saying yea to oneself, of taking oneself as the most serious
> of tasks, of being conscious of everything one does, and
> keeping it constantly before one's eyes in all its dubious
> aspects—truly a task that taxes us to the utmost. (CW 13,
> para. 24)

In the course of this study, we have talked much about
the need to turn and relate to the various contents of the
unconscious as they present themselves to consciousness.

This is one of the major points of having to suffer through the inferior function and the subsequent toppling of the ego's position of dominance in the psyche.

But outside of being initiated into that larger *mysterium tremendum* of which we each seem to be a part, what is left to do? That is, once one goes through a decisive experience with the inferior function and has had an intimation of the archetypal Self, how can one foster a relationship that reflects and develops the experience? "Real increase of personality," Jung tells us, "means consciousness of an enlargement that flows from inner sources . . . a man grows with the greatness of his task" (CW 9ii, para 215). But how does one go about measuring up to the task; how does one do one's "duty" to one's Self?

First, one must take oneself seriously. Because consciousness in the West is generally oriented through an elevation of the object over the subject and an idolization of the thinking function, all Westerners have an additional barrier to cross in getting through to themselves. Overcoming this barrier seems requisite to even beginning to see or realize one's psychological type. As we have seen with Jung himself, typology can be an extremely helpful tool in finding one's bearings.

Second, one must take the unconscious seriously. This, as we have said, is the point of the inferior function—which acts as a kind of cruel and insidious initiation into the unconscious and the Self. As the inferior function is part of each of our individual psychological types, we should not expect it to go away. It is with us always, like the unconscious itself, ever ready to remind us about what we would rather control, repress, or forget. Each psychological type must gather the courage to risk close contact with this dark side of the personality in a way that does not presume the dominance of the conscious functions or the bias and saving graces of the collective. This in turn will give the individual a "readiness" to experience the reality of the psyche and the archetypal Self.

Third, one must make an effort to learn the language of the unconscious, the language of symbols. The symbol for Jung is always the product of something very complex in the psyche. Symbols are the means by which the psyche unites any opposites that otherwise would have torn it apart. In this regard, Jung calls the symbol a *coincidentia oppositorium* or a *tertium*, an irrational "third" thing that has the capacity to creatively nurture all the important issues that the psyche needs to draw on to sustain itself as well as to grow in knowledge of itself.

Fourth, one must come to know the source of this symbol-making activity in the psyche. This means exercising for oneself what Jung calls "the transcendent function."[2] Because of its importance in rounding out our understanding of typology in the context of Jungian psychology, we will now deal with this peculiar "fifth," or "quintessential," function in some detail.

Jung himself uses the term "transcendent function" to designate the means by which consciousness moves into an "area" or "realm" in the psyche that he refers to as the "middle ground." This is hypothetically an area in which neither consciousness nor the unconscious has unfair advantage over the other. It exists *in potentia* as a field of opportunities for the personality to effect a temporary collaboration between two normally combative sides of the psyche. The transcendent function both acts in and gives rise to this proverbial "middle realm." One could in turn view this "middle ground" or "middle realm" as the natural birthplace of the symbol.

In the "middle realm," the question for the individual becomes, in good Heraclitian fashion, how to find the greatest harmony out of the greatest tension, i.e., how consciousness must relate to the unconscious without trying to dictate or dominate it, and, as importantly, without the unconscious itself taking over the personality. Jung warns us:

> The conscious mind allows itself to be trained like a parrot, but the unconscious does not—which is why St. Augustine thanked God for not making him responsible for his dreams. The unconscious is a psychic fact; any efforts to drill it are only apparently successful, and moreover harmful to consciousness. It is and remains beyond the reach of subjective arbitrary control, a realm where nature and her secrets can neither be improved upon nor perverted, where we can listen but may not meddle. (Jacobi, 1953, p. 26)

If one's experience with the inferior function has been decisive, the listening process has already begun. The ego, realizing it is no longer at the center of the psyche, willingly acknowledges its attachment to something "other," to the Self, about which it moves.

This in effect allows consciousness itself more "mobility" to explore the psyche, to roam around the center rather than straining to keep the center for itself. Specifically in regard to one's psychological type, von Franz describes the situation insightfully.

> The problem of the functions is no longer relevant. The functions have become instruments of a consciousness which is no longer rooted in them or driven by them. (1984, p. 63)

The activity or ability of consciousness that comes with the dislocation of the ego is in fact the transcendent function operating in the "middle realm" and involving the individual in a new attitude in which consciousness itself can be placed at service to the unconscious.

Jung warns that putting consciousness at the disposal of the unconscious can be a risky affair and should not be treated in a cavalier manner (CW 8, pp. 67–68). But he likewise comments that "individuation is closely connected with the *transcendent function*" (CW 6, para. 759), and goes on to detail how one may participate in this "middle realm" (CW 8, paras. 131–193). We may summarize the procedure as it may relate to an encounter with the inferior function as follows.

Consciousness first begins by making a concentrated movement to meet whatever the inferior function has latched onto. For example, should an introverted thinking-type be experiencing inferior extraverted feeling, the person would devote his or her attention to the external object and the affect or mood which seemingly comes from the object. This means stepping down off one's "high horse," where so often the inferior function places consciousness, and approaching the affect without hysteria or malice. (One recalls Nietzsche's line "bad love to yourself makes solitude a prison.") Approaching the affect and object in this way provides an opening and legitimacy for any unconscious material that may be trying to make its way up to consciousness.

Next, fantasy, a natural attribute of the unconscious, is allowed the freest play in regard to the object. Jung cautions that this is not to be confused with Freud's method of "free association." For Jung, Freud's technique takes the person too far afield from both the mood and the object, thereby missing an important connection which the unconscious has already made for consciousness. Also, "free association" has a tendency to keep the person "passive" or at the mercy of the unconscious, and so does not represent a true *conscious* collaboration with it.

Comparing the two approaches, Jung refers to the tendency of Freud's method to float the person backward to past complexes, eventually leading the individual to a reductive relationship with or understanding of the unconscious. Jung's own method focuses more on the present and future and leads the individual to what he terms a constructive-synthetic relationship with the unconscious (CW 6, paras. 701–788).

A phrase which is used almost interchangeably with the transcendent function and is perhaps more descriptive of what is taking place in these regards is "active imagination."[3] Active imagination conveys the sense that the conscious individual is actually *working with* the unconscious. Jung also describes active imagination as "this little matter of living in a metaphor" or "dreaming with your eyes open."

When Jung is explaining the technique of active imagination, it is not unusual for him to urge the unconscious to speak directly on the matter at hand, as if there were a person in the unconscious who could talk for the mood or affect or image under consideration. Jung advises, "get the mood to speak to him; his mood must tell him all about itself and show him through what kind of fantastic analogies it is expressing itself" (CW 7, para. 348). This involvement of consciousness increases the possibility of an ongoing dialogue with the unconscious and leaves the future open for further exploration of the psyche.

As this effort is taking place, Jung also instructs that the individual further cooperate with the unconscious by writing down everything arising from the unconscious in as clear and noncritical a manner as possible. According to him,

> The whole procedure is a kind of enrichment and clarification of the affect, whereby the affect and its contents are brought nearer to consciousness, becoming at the same time more impressive and more understandable. (CW 8, para. 167)

If an actual dialogue is to take place between consciousness and the unconscious, one would make the additional effort to write down what happens on both sides of the exchange.

In his essay on the transcendent function (CW 8, paras. 131–193), Jung also suggests drawing, painting, sculpting, or dance as other possible ways to creatively give form and relate to the unconsciousness. One would first select the medium with which one has a certain talent and feels most comfortable, and then proceed as described above.

Because a specific medium may be involved, one may be tempted to believe that when one engages in active imagination one is producing "art." However, a person does not enter into active imagination with any intention of producing a work of art. The idea is to allow the unconscious a relatively safe place to play with consciousness and to see what comes out of the encounter when both sides of the personality are treated equally and fairly.

In regard to any drawing or painting that comes from active imagination, Jung comments:

> It is not important for the picture to be technically or aesthetically satisfying, but merely for fantasy to have free play and for the whole thing to be done as well as possible. (CW 8, para. 168)

Though the production may not be a "work of art," we are nonetheless dealing here with something that is at the source of both art and culture, namely, the symbol-making activities of the psyche. It then makes sense to ask whether what is produced is in fact a symbol.

Jung tells us that what makes a symbol depends chiefly on the "attitude of the observing consciousness" (CW 6, para. 818). The symbol for Jung is the best possible expression of something relatively unknown but that is nonetheless alive and "pregnant with meaning" (CW 6, para. 817). These are the key features: aliveness and meaning-full-ness. It is feasible that through active imagination one can produce such a symbol.

The effect of such a symbol on the personality is generally positive and healing. Once the mood or affect has been given some kind of image and form, the negative energy from the unconscious that was working disruptively or destructively against the ego is effectively withdrawn from the unconscious and moved over to the symbol. The symbol converts negative energy into something which the personality itself can respond to in a positive way.

In some instances, the individual may produce something that serves not only as a symbol for him or herself, but that may move the collective in just such a powerful way. This makes such a symbol important to look at it in terms of what it may or may not have to say about the individuals it serves. Jung now comments,

> Whether or not such symbols will have a limited or general social validity depends on the viability of the creative individual. The more abnormal, i.e., the less viable he is, the more limited will be the social validity of the symbols he produces, though their value may be absolute for the individual himself. (CW 6, para. 720)

Needless to say, the criterion of "viability" that Jung sets up here for the "social validity" of a symbol in relation to the individual producing it is highly problematic. Yet implicit in his comment is a warning that should be heeded. Because one is dealing with the unconscious, one should be on guard against being "duped" into making too much or too little of any product emerging from active imagination. Oddly enough, it is the person who most believes that his or her symbol is "speaking for thousands" who usually has little to say to anyone but him- or herself.

The true test of a symbol which represents the collective is in its own liveliness and meaningfulness apart from the individual. That is, symbols work powerfully on their own without anyone insisting on their importance. When doing active imagination, the most important thing remains simply that one produce something tangible that can reflect the collaboration between consciousness and the unconscious.

Here again, however, it may also be said that the transcendent function is somewhere at the source of much of what we would term culture, insofar as culture has an influence on our lives. The connection to what we have been talking about can now be made through what Johan Huizinga has analyzed as the spirit of play. In Huizinga's perceptive study, *Homo Ludens*, he calls attention to what may be thought of as some of the more "socially valid" results of "the transcendent function." A brief paragraph from this wildly variegated work must suffice:

> Our point of departure must be the conception of an almost childlike play-sense, expressing itself in various play-forms, some serious, some playful, but all rooted in ritual and productive of culture by allowing the innate human need of rhythm, harmony, change, alternation, contrast, and climax, etc., to unfold in full richness. Coupled with this play-sense is a spirit that strives for honor, dignity, superiority, and beauty. Magic and mystery, heroic longing, and the foreshadowings of music, sculpture, and logic all seek form and expression in noble play. (1955, p. 75)

Huizinga addresses the odd mix of ego-Self relations that we have been speaking about, and expresses great respect for the powerful unconscious currents that one would expect to find in any genuine symbolic activity. In addition, Huizinga links the "play-element" to a "childlikeness" that most of us can easily relate to when doing active imagination. This of course does not take anything away from the seriousness of "play."

Not surprisingly, Jung has referred to the child archetype as the ideal "formula for the symbol" (CW 9i, para. 291), a kind of symbol for symbols. The child archetype is privileged this way in Jung's pantheon of archetypes because it represents, as it does for Huizinga, the emergence into consciousness of the symbol-making activities of the psyche itself, of the irrational and new coming into existence through the ordered image.

Regardless of the role of the transcendent function in art

or culture, its place in the life of the individual cannot be contested. Working with the transcendent function as it arose in his own life as well as his clinical work with patients, Jung finally concluded that the conscious realization and experience of fantasies through the procedure of active imagination "has far reaching consequences itself" (CW 7, para. 359), consequences which are nothing less than the eventual reestablishment of the self-regulating tendencies of the psyche (CW 8, para. 165).

Analysts who have followed Jung's lead in this regard have gone on to corroborate his findings. They have observed that often it is only through the transcendent function or active imagination that we can pick up sufficiently on the clues which the unconscious gives to consciousness on a regular basis. Von Franz goes so far as to say that "active imagination is practically the only way of dealing with the fourth function" (1984, p. 63). Aniela Jaffé believes that "creativity comes alive when consciousness allies itself with the inferior function" (1984, p. 111). Both analysts are saying, in effect, that the role of the transcendent function in dealing with the inferior function, indeed in dealing with the unconscious, should not be underestimated.[4]

This brief introduction to the possible place of the transcendent function in a person's life is meant to be more a description of than a prescription for relating to the unconscious, a tricky affair to say the least. If nothing else, it highlights by contrast the manner in which we normally snub the unconscious as it comes into our lives. The transcendent function, if we let it, can link us back to the unconscious in such a way that the power of the Self begins to resonate meaningfully in one's life and soul. Problems are solved or changes take place that would otherwise be inhibited by the hypertrophy of our everyday consciousness. In the end, this makes whatever effort we make with the transcendent function not only necessary but worthwhile.

Notes

1. The archetypal images which Jung terms the *anima* and the *animus* together form a critical part of Jung's psychology. In tradi-

tional Jungian psychology, the anima and animus represent the contrasexual influences from the unconscious on the conscious personalities of the male and female, respectively. Specifically, anima/us are archetypal compensations for the *persona*. See CW 6, paras. 797–811.

As archetypes, the anima and animus have both positive and negative features which consciousness would have to come to terms with in order to claim any serious level of relationship to the unconscious.

This area of Jungian psychology requires extensive treatment to get anywhere near the mark. There are over six hundred citations for the anima/animus in Jung's *Collected Works*. Further helpful citations include: CW 7, paras. 296–340, CW 9ii, paras. 20–42, CW 9i, paras. 111–147. Significant book-length studies include the following: Hillman, J. (1986). *Anima*. Dallas: Spring Publications; Ulanov, A. B. (1971). *The Feminine in Jungian Psychology and in Christian Theology*. Evanston: Northwestern University Press; Whitmont, E. C. (1986). *Return of the Goddess*. New York: Crossroad; Jung, E. (1957). *Anima and Animus*. Dallas: Spring Publications.

2. On references to the transcendent function in Jung's *Collected Works* which were used in this summary, see especially the following: CW 8, paras. 131–193; CW 6, paras. 318–374; CW 7, paras. 778–781.

3. On specific references to active imagination in the works of Jung, sell Hull, R. F. C. (1971). "Bibliographic notes on active imagination in the works of C. G. Jung" (pp. 115–120), in *Spring 1971*. Current book-length studies on this topic include Hannah, B. (1981), *Encounters with the Soul: Active Imagination*; and Johnson, R. A. (1986), *Inner Work*.

Relating to the unconscious is of course the *raison d'etre* for Jungian psychology. For an excellent review of the different methods used in analysis to connect the conscious and unconscious life of the individual, see Stein, M. (ed.) (1984), *Jungian Analysis*, pp. 123–234.

4. Anyone truly interested in knowing how the transcendent function works and its importance in Jung's thinking must eventually tackle his researches on alchemy (CW 12, 13, & 14). Jung comments,

> The secret of alchemy was in fact the transcendent function, the transformation of the personality through the blending and fusion of the noble with the base components, of the differentiated with the inferior functions, of the conscious with the unconscious. (CW 7, para. 360)

VI

Type Development and the Individuation Process

In the last analysis, every life is the realization of a whole, that is, of a Self, for which reason this realization can also be called 'individuation.'

(CW 12, para. 330)

My life is a story of the self-realization of the unconscious.

opening sentence to
Memories, Dreams, Reflections

It is of the utmost importance in practical treatment to keep the goal of the individual's development constantly in view.

(CW 7, para. 462)

I AM FULLY AWARE that this chapter smacks of presumption. However, in doing workshops on typology, specifically on typology and the individuation process, questions of type development inevitably come up. I am providing what I have come to understand about type development as "work in progress" and would not want these very provisional thoughts to appear as too structured or dogmatic, especially in regard to the developmental schema suggested below.

Two further warnings seem in order in this regard. First, whenever one talks about development of any kind, there is a tendency to want to fit individuals into one stage or another, and measure their progress against a standard that is implied as "normal" and "right" for the age of the individual in question. As has been my intention throughout this work, I am seeking more to put Jung's typology back into the larger context of his work as a whole. Approaching the issue of type development is important to me primarily in this sense. Though I will have recourse to set out a stage theory in regard to age and type development, what follows is meant primarily to translate much of what one can read in Jung's later works concerning the individuation process itself back into typological concepts and language; that is, whatever is said in regard to stages and ages is not meant to suggest one linear path of "normal" development.

Warning #2: It is true that Jung went far beyond typology as he sought more and more to come to terms with the various aspects of the psyche as a whole. It is also true that there is a richness in Jung's latter, more imagistic works that certainly may be lost if what follows is simply an attempt to stuff all of Jung's depth psychology into his typology or into notions of type development. Neither is that my intention.

However, I believe Jung admits late in his life to never abandoning his typology for good reason. In fact, all of Jung's writings can be viewed as of a piece, meaning that there is an underlying unity to Jung's work and vision. Reading the twenty-plus volumes of the *Collected Works* teaches us, if nothing else, how wonderfully gifted Jung was at saying the same or similar things in a variety of ways and from a variety of angles.

This justifies us in approaching typological development as a variation on a main theme, i.e., as a specific and provocative angle or approach to a problem that obsessed Jung throughout his life: "What does it mean to individuate?"

Setting the Stage

Type development is a refinement of ego-consciousness developing out of the unconscious. Before looking at type development specifically, we must set the stage for what happens between the unconscious and ego-consciousness, more generally speaking.

For Jung an individual's consciousness, though shaped by time, culture, and the unique elements particular to the personality itself, grows out of what he viewed as the virtually timeless, transcultural matrix of the unconscious; that is, the unconscious, as an autonomous and independent factor was, early on in Jung's career, considered to be the "mother" to consciousness.

This deceptively simple idea was revolutionary when it was first decisively purported by Jung, during his break from Freud in 1912. The unconscious, said Jung, was not simply a repository of repressed, unwanted memories and emotions cast off in the course of one's early psychosexual development, thereafter to infiltrate and frustrate future living—as Freud's work suggested. Such a pessimistic drama certainly could be viewed as a significant aspect of unconscious processes in general, and was indeed referred to by Jung under the rubric of the *personal* unconscious.

But the unconscious likewise included a plethora of *archetypal* aspects that transcended one's personal biography, and tangled one up even more dramatically and meaningfully in the development and history of the human species as a whole. It was the *archetypes,* a few of which we have had occasion to mention in this study (shadow, anima/animus, Self), that would hold Jung's lifelong attention and establish the richness of his larger psychological model. These particularly compelling, transpersonal, transcultural configurations of psychic energy were brought together by Jung in their myriad and interrelated forms under the rubric of what he termed the *collective* unconscious or the "objective psyche."

By this one insight or discovery (i.e., the recognition of the *collective* unconscious, from which the *personal* unconscious itself took its ultimate significance), the potential for growth in consciousness increased 1,000-fold. In fact, given this discovery, it would make sense to consider the kind and quality of consciousness potentially now available to individuals to be itself a new phenomenon in its own right.

By viewing the unconscious as the matrix to consciousness (and against Freudian reductionism), Jungian psychology theoretically gives individual consciousness the opportunity, even duty, to realize its connection and relationship to the unconscious as a whole. With Jung's formulation of the collective unconscious, one is now capable of being in a genuinely reciprocal relationship to what would be once thought of metaphysically as beyond oneself in scope and power, space and time, or what would be viewed scientifically as nonsense.

Jung's text *Psychological Types* has been criticized and sometimes dismissed by some Jungians for being too conceptual and for ignoring "complex" theory, which was the precursor to Jung's fuller understanding of the archetypal basis of the psyche, referred to above. The excitement many feel when talking about Jung's larger psychological model and the energy that is generated in relating to specific, archetypal patterns of the collective unconscious seem to some to be missing in Jung's typological work, or in talk about typology.

I believe these criticisms to be shortsighted and largely unfair. The main archetypal problematic which Jung is evolving in his work on *Types* focuses on the archetypal Self, and the complex that Jung is discussing throughout his text is the ego-complex. This is a tremendously exciting and interesting problematic he is working on, nothing less than the ego-Self constellation. Jung does not put it quite this way (the conceptual apparatus is not yet fully available to him), but all the evidence is there in his original 1920 text, even if in sometimes disguised or embryonic form.

By 1928, eight years after his book on *Types* appeared and when virtually all the pieces of Jung's model were conceptually in place, Jung would have clearly developed the hypothesis that one particular archetype, the archetypal Self, acted as the superordinate factor in the psyche, around which the personality itself took shape.

We have already seen how the archetypal Self figured into encounters with the inferior function, and how in turn an experience with the Self can totally change one's orientation to inner and outer life, providing a new center from which to tether one's life.

The Self, represented mythologically by various God-images, mandala configurations, or centering symbols was considered, in Jung's psychology as a whole, as a functional analogue to God, who, psychologically speaking, was ultimately ineffable. While God him/herself was a metaphysical problem that Jung as an empiricist tried to walk around, God as a psychological experience was always a legitimate concern of his that he expressed through his considerable research and work on manifestations of the archetypal Self.

It was a supreme paradox to Jung that type development, as an aspect of ego-consciousness, often involved the individual's ego differentiating itself from the unconscious, and from the Self, to such a degree that the ego seemed to work *against* the personality as a whole, i.e., against the Self. In the process of differentiating a function and attitude-type, the ego often ended up alienated from the source of its own being as well as in conflict with other egos doing the same thing. We will have much more to say about this shortly.

Jung was also amazed and confounded at how clever and creative individuals could be in separating themselves from the unconscious as well as in marking themselves off from one another. Much *good*, it would seem, can also come from individuals acting on their typological biases. This problem of differences and of differentiation is a significant part of Jung's work on types.

But, as we approach an understanding of type development and the individuation process, we must always bear in mind that Jung was firmly convinced that the unconscious itself was a primary factor in its own right, interacting creatively with ego-consciousness as the personality evolved. This is the approach we have taken in this study.

The unconscious and the archetypal Self were then likely to be making ongoing contributions of one kind or another to one's individual psychological development and personhood, regardless of the ego's position along the way. In fact, in many instances these "contributions" were of a nature that could be unpredictable or upsetting by ego standards alone, though when viewed in the context of Jung's larger model, could likewise be understood as part of the the self-regulatory action of the psyche as a whole.

For Jung type development was not simply what the ego would do to differentiate itself from the unconscious and from others, which relates to the problem of differentiation and the problem of differences. Type development would also emphasize the problem of opposites. And the problem of opposites could be represented in one of its most intense and dramatic forms as a conflict between the ego, as the center and carrier of consciousness, and the Self, as the center and circumference of the personality as a whole.

To reiterate: in our understanding of type development, the archetypal Self will always be somewhere in the picture, in some vague form or stage of emergence, during the course of an individual's life. That is, type development, as a sub-category of ego functioning, is regulated in some sense by the archetypal Self, however unnerving, problematic, and paradoxical that may seem to the ego at any one time.

Beyond the trash bin of the Freudian unconscious, Jung's psychology opened the way to view and experience what once only madmen, religious prophets, and poets dared to speak about (i.e., the unconscious in its most powerful and divergent aspects, the workings of the archetypal Self), and to give it in part at least a provisional home, or place of recognition, in consciousness. This approach to unconscious material was truly revolutionary and liberating.

In order to handle this experience, however, the ego must be first differentiated out of the unconscious. Once this happens, an opposition then takes place between consciousness and the unconscious. As the ego achieves a certain strength and status, it empowers consciousness, often at the expense of the unconscious.

If the ego pulls too far away from the unconscious, the unconscious, in the spirit of wholeness, will have its "revenge." Action taken by the archetypal Self seeks to restore a healthier balance between conscious and unconscious life. If all goes well, around midlife, if not earlier, the narrow ego is displaced in favor of something larger than itself, and acquires an awareness which provides a new center to the personality as a whole. This new center is now the "place" from which the ego derives its energy for the future.

The ultimate return in this arrangement for consciousness is a sense of rootedness, meaning, and an intimation of wholeness that goes beyond personal existence, or "egohood" as such. In this way, Jungian psychology makes possible a quantum leap in enhancing the possibilities of consciousness itself, of which type development plays its part.

Ego-Self Connections

Before one is able to truly grasp the significance of the profound connection and interrelationship possible between conscious and unconscious life, between ego and Self, one seems to have to undergo at least two major "death" experiences, alluded to above.

First, the emerging and fragile ego, representing consciousness, pulls itself out and away from the unconscious, the matrix. In so doing, the personality loses or distorts the natural connection it would have to its source. It does this through differentiating itself from the unconscious. If we could avoid romanticizing childhood too much, one could use the metaphor of "Paradise Lost" to convey this first "death experience."

Second, once the ego breaks away from the unconscious and achieves a certain status and power, usually peaking in the first half of life, it is called to give itself back to the archetypal Self from which it had pulled away. As we have seen, this occurs in small but decisive ways whenever one has a true encounter with the inferior function. And it occurs in a big way for most during midlife, the transition to the second half of life.

As the personality develops then, there seem to be two different agendas for the two halves of life, with midlife itself as a pronounced and prolonged liminal state in between these two halves (see Stein, 1983). These different agendas would naturally impact any understanding of type development.

In his essay "Stages of Life" (CW 8, 1930), Jung uses the metaphor of the morning sun rising out of darkness, stretching its rays out over the land in powerful and definitive ways as it reaches the noon hour. At last, the sun reaches a point when, first imperceptibly and later more remarkably, the rays begin to pull back, shrink, or go in retreat. Twilight and darkness begin to get the upper hand again. This twilight state, analogous to the midlife transition, separates the two life agendas. The sun in this context represents ego-consciousness.

Jung's special twist on this metaphor is that he suggests that the rays of the sun in the second half of life do not simply disappear from the face of the earth, making old age meaningless, i.e., simply a failure of the life urge or a decline of youthful vigor and purpose. The rays of the sun as twilight and darkness take over actually withdraw back into the individual's inner life, to his or her own soul, in order to now provide illumination from within.

In this metaphor, then, Jung is saying that the first half of life is clearly about ego development, and consciousness extending out. The second half of life is more about a recog-

nition of the connection between ego and Self, and consciousness turning in.

It seems that the ego must first move from a place of relative weakness (dawn) to a place of relative strength (noon).
And, later, the ego must be willing to sacrifice its primacy or
centeredness (twilght) to give way to the Self (death). The ego
in effect has to establish itself as the would-be King of the
personality, the "false" center, before a genuinely full, conscious realization of the psyche as a whole becomes possible,
which becomes the task left mostly to the second half of life,
culminating in one's physical death.

Following the metaphor along, type development would
primarily and obviously focus first on establishing the ego as
"King" (or "Queen") through differentiating the ego from the
unconscious. Once the ego claims its place, defining itself in
specific typological dimensions, life in the proverbial "real
world" goes "forward" and "outward." Preferences are now
more freely accented, and the will is exerted to maintain the
ego's precarious position against the unconscious from which
it emerged and with the outer world to which it is held
accountable. One can readily see how power and control continue to be major ego-issues in this first-half-of-life agenda.

As alluded to earlier, many achievements and accomplishments come from this kind of seemingly inevitable
hubris or arrogance, achievements from which we have all
benefited. Furthermore, given the first-half-of-life agenda, we
would be hard-pressed to be overly critical of what the ego is
trying to attain, even with its often one-sided and ambitious
maneuvering. The ego wants to provide confidence, continuity, stability, purpose, control, and a safe knowledge base for
the emerging personality facing the inner and outer worlds.

One feature in this picture seems clear: type development
and ego-formation are definitely interrelated; that is, developing preferences for introversion or extraversion, sensing,
intuiting, thinking, or feeling seems to provide the ego with
the broad lines that define its nature and help to maintain its
consistency in behavior, continuity in time, and place in the
"real" world.

What, one might ask, could be happening along the way
between type development in the ego and the archetypal Self?
As mentioned earlier, the archetypal Self is never far away in

type development and ego-formation, so let us now start translating the archetypal Self into typological terms.

Stages of Type Development

By the representation below I want to suggest that the archetypal Self includes everything one could imagine from a typological perspective; that is, the Self includes both introverted and extraverted attitudes as well as all four functions (sensing, intuiting, thinking, and feeling), and all possible combinations of attitudes and functions. This is, strictly speaking, a typological version or metaphor of the archetypal Self, represented as a totality or mandala symbol, which functions to bring together and order the disparate facts and facets of ego-functioning in the context of typology.

Archetypal Self

$$I_N^F \qquad\qquad E_N^F$$
$$\rule{0.5pt}{100pt}$$
$$I_T^S \qquad\qquad E_T^S$$

I certainly am not saying that this rendering is the only way to represent the Self or even the best way. But, as a symbol of totality for the subject at hand, typology or type development, this representation does the trick. It transcends any one thing that we could say about a particular individual in regard to type and gets us to the starting point we need to look at type development more closely.

Now, for purposes of looking at type development, we

would want to view this version of the archetypal Self as incipient within the infant being born. No typological qualities would be clearly differentiated in the infant's immediate experience. Everything in the infant's experience would be a vivid panoply of colors and forms, forces and influences, instincts and archetypes, in which inner and outer life would be very difficult to distinguish.

We would want to assume then a measure of fluidity and chaos that the infant experiences in regard to the Self. Potential typological aspects of the emerging ego may be conflicting with one another, or fighting to differentiate out from the *massa confusa* that depicts the undifferentiated whole. Or, later on, different embryonic aspects of one's type may be evoked appropriately or not in the course of an infant's development.

And yet, during all of this, one imagines that there would be "something" that is working in the infant's behalf to get it to develop on a number of levels (physical, mental, spiritual, and emotional), moving it along, within and without, providing the patterning he or she needs to grow. This growth or maturing of the personality would include also the development of an ego central to consciousness itself.

The "something" mentioned above, in the Jungian sense, is the combined effort of the archetypes themselves, mediated by what the infant encounters in the environment, especially one's own parents. Specifically, however, in regard to ego development and the individual's life as a whole, the main archetype in question is the archetypal Self.

The schema on pages 152 and 153 illustrates a typical course of development, using an introverted feeling-type with extraverted intuition as a "goal" of ego-development. From what has been said and shown in these illustrations, I view type-development in four stages, with what may be referred to as pre- and post-stages that are in themselves qualitatively different than the intervening four stages relating specifically to ego-formation.

The *pre-stage* marks the existence of the archetypal Self and the collective unconscious prior to an individual's birth. When someone is born, that person in not simply born into a physical world of people and things, but rather is born into a psychological world, an archetypal world, as well. Or, as Jung was fond of saying, "we are not born a *tabula rasa.*"

The task ahead of the personality is for the emerging ego to establish itself with some strength in regard to what becomes the inner and outer worlds. That process is what more specifically is illustrated by the four stages. It is especially important that the emerging personality not remain lost to the archetypal world alone. If the archetypal world could be thought of metaphorically as the world of Gods and Goddesses (see, for example, Bolen, 1984, 1989), one could say that the infant growing out and away from the unconscious must gradually be "humanized," taken out of the world dominated by the Gods and Goddesses and into the world of people and culture at large (a movement from the sacred to the profane, so to speak).

A consequence of this pulling away in our culture is that as the ego gets stronger, the Gods and Goddesses *seem* to get weaker. However, Jung would insist on this occurrence as only "seeming" to be so. To paraphrase Jung, the Gods and Goddesses have not disappeared at all as the ego gets stronger; they have simply gone into the unconscious, where they set up neurotic patterns of behavior that can encroach and tyrannize over the conscious personality, without the individual's awareness. In fact, insofar as the ego is successful in becoming "liberated" (split off) from the archetypal world, it runs the risk of an *enantiodromia,* itself becoming a "God" or "Goddess" in an unconscious way.

Type development then serves to position the ego as the would-be "King" (or "Queen") of the personality, while bringing it into the quintessentially human world. Amazingly enough, this is done in most cases more or less successfully, though one could argue, not without everyone ending up neurotic to some degree or another. Why is this the case, one may ask?

Fortunately or not, in this process of ego development, neither the ego wins completely nor the archetypal world. It seems true that the human and the divine cannot be totally split apart. In fact, psychologically speaking, there is a preponderance of evidence that suggests we are truly born "in the image and likeness of God," in spite of the ego's hubris, or however acute type development may be in the first half of

Jung's Psychology of Consciousness

Individual Typology

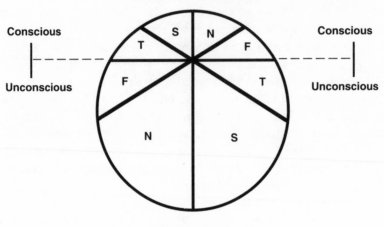

Birth to Age 6

Functions emerging into consciousness;
all preferences developing

Sample: Introverted Feeling

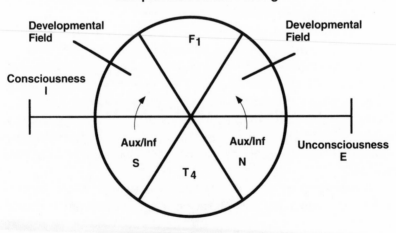

6 to 12 Years

Superior function helps to define ego;
other preferences developing

Sample: Introverted Feeling

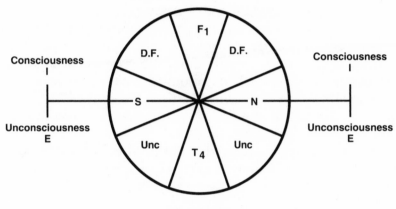

12 to 20 Years

Superior function still defines ego. Problem of opposites introduced via auxiliary functions. Success measured by differentiation of one auxiliary function serving ego.

Sample: Introverted Feeling, Extraverted Intuition

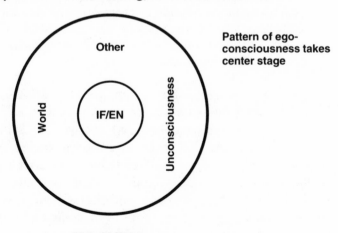

Pattern of ego-consciousness takes center stage

20 to 35 Years

Superior function and one auxiliary function in opposite attitude establishes ego as center of consciousness; ego can now mimic archetypal Self life. This fact makes for all the possible encroachments and entanglements from the unconscious as well as what is creative and life affirming in the personality as a whole.

All along the way of type development and ego-formation, we find the personal and the transpersonal, the ego and the Self, consciousness and the unconscious, complexes and archetypes, constantly mixing. In this scenario most egos actually do well to differentiate one function in one attitude, e.g., introverted feeling. This amounts to a modern version of the proverbial "hero's journey." So, whatever "bad" one may speak of the ego, it should take into account what the ego itself has "been through."

The *post-stage* could be thought of as going significantly beyond type development as part of ego-formation, and references more and more the work one does with the inferior function (see Chapter IV).

In Jung's *Collected Papers*, published in 1917, as he was sorting through his understanding of the inferior function and the individuation process, and was himself still within his own "confrontation with the unconscious," he comments:

> The development of the contrary function that was hitherto unconscious leads to individuation beyond the type and thereby to a new relation to the world and mind. (*Collected Papers*, "The Psychology of the Unconscious Process," [a revised and expanded version of "New Paths in Psychology," 1916], 1917, p. 441).

This post-stage refers then to the relationship that becomes possible between conscious and unconscious life when the ego itself is displaced and put in service to the archetypal Self. At this stage, ideally, the transcendent function (see Chapter V, pp. 130–138) kicks in on a regular basis to shape one's life. This virtually means that the individual's life is no longer "ego-driven," and that all four functions take on new meaning in the context of relating to the whole. Interestingly, Jung's essay on the transcendent function was written in 1916, though it was not published until 1958.

To sum up: If the task of consciousness in the first half of life is to establish its own center, referred by Jung as the ego or ego-complex, it would seem that the infant is off to a rocky start at best. The infant has no ego, no center of consciousness to speak of. This is not to say some form of awareness is not operating, but it is most likely brought to the infant via the archetypes, and mediated through the parents and the world "out there." This insight would explain both the incredible forms that "infant knowledge" takes as well as the liveliness, energy, and wonder which infancy and childhood represent to adults. Jung would say that significant unconscious forces (the archetypes) are at play in moving the infant along, which are themselves necessary to the life process as a whole, i.e., throughout all of life. This is all capsulized when Jung says that we are not born a *tabula rasa*. But, as importantly, we are not born an ego either. And there's the rub.

In addition to the various archetypal forces helping the infant along, Jung posits a superordinate force in the unconscious that has a teleological effect on the developing personality. There is in effect something ahead of the infant to pull it along, forward, into the light of day, into consciousness itself, into ego, ultimately into who and what the individual personality must be. This force, or configuration of psychic energy, is posited by Jung as the archetypal Self, of which the ego, when finally developed, is a poor though necessary imitation.

It is as if the Self, along with managing the development of the personality from behind the scenes, sends out at birth a small, cryptic piece of itself, the emerging ego, to make its way in the world. As that piece develops, the Self moves more and more from what is unknown, unreal, incipient, and unexperienced by the infant to what eventually is more known, more real, and ideally better integrated by the developing personality. In this sense the emerging ego and the Self need each other.

Of course, such an ideal course of development never occurs. An optimal connection between ego and Self is seldom the case in growing up. The world, culture, family, and a myriad of other factors can corrupt or frustrate the developing personality, knocking it off its proverbial "path," or even severing its connection to the Self.

Type development is perhaps the most significant aspect of ego-development as the personality matures. For Jung the first half of life seemed unequivocally and properly devoted to type development as part of ego-consciousness separating from the unconscious. The ego must differentiate itself, mark itself off in effective ways, to manage both inner and outer worlds.

We have seen too, however, that commonly the tables turn when at midlife type development involves the eventual sacrifice of the ego's reign back to the archetypal Self, the source and eventual end of the ego's individual being. The sun begins to set, or in Jung's provocative metaphor, it turns its rays to the inside. With this change, the agenda for living the rest of one's life changes, the problem of opposites becomes more imposing and significant. And in order to "solve" such a problem one finds oneself moving now more toward archetypal reality in (ideally) conscious and willing ways.

Midlife itself seems to be a protracted encounter of unconscious material, a twilight period for confronting unlived life, i.e., all those elements of psyche left out during ego-formation and development. Indeed, midlife is something of a "haunting" of consciousness by the unconscious.

Finally, we have seen too that this midlife phenomenon occurs as well in smaller though potentially decisive ways, through fateful encounters with the inferior function.

Type development is not simply a linear model going from point *A* to *Z*, as may have been implied by our earlier diagrams. Rather, it is ultimately a way to establish the ego and prepare the individual to enter into the inner world of psyche itself. In that inner world of psyche, one is more prone to circumambulation, as the Jungians are fond of saying, circling around a new center, looking at and experiencing the core of the personality as a whole, and as world as well. In this way, the archetypal Self makes itself known to consciousness. Eventually, Jung himself comments, "The process of development proves on closer inspections to be cyclic or spiral" (CW 12, para. 186).

In 1935 in a lecture on typology given at Tavistock to a room of about two hundred medical doctors, Jung made use of terminology that may be helpful to rounding off our understanding of type development. Jung posits two fields with which the emerging personality must reckon. The *ectopsy-*

chic field is what would be taken as the visible, tangible world that requires our immediate attention and involvement. For all practical purposes it is the "real" world, established by the senses and shared more or less by others, and the world in which the developing ego is tethered in the first half of life. It is here where Jung believes his psychology of consciousness, his typology, primarily focuses.

Then there is the *endopsychic* field, which is the realm where Jung postulates that the more unconscious (invisible, intangible, unaware) processes reside. Its contents include subjective components of conscious functions, whatever is unsaid or left out from the ectopsychic field, unadapted behaviors, unseemly emotions or affective events, states of possession, and unconscious invasions. In a word it is the unconscious as shadow, and the eventual world in which the ego must face and own, as part of the second-half-of-life development.

In our culture type development in the first half of life relating to the ectopsychic field is rewarded. For individuals whose superior function is extraverted, the ectopsychic world initially poses less a problem (and perhaps greater rewards) than for those individuals whose superior function is introverted. Introverts would tend to be maladapted, or view themselves as maladapted, to the ectopsychic field, and perhaps experience the first half of life in a more "tortuous" or at least tentative fashion.

What seems to me to be even more often the case, introverts overadapt their extraverted, auxiliary function. They take their encounter with the ectopsychic world seriously by devaluing their introverted preference and adapting with their extraverted preference. Whatever happens, one insight has become extremely clear to me in my clinical work: while we could say minimally that both introverts and extraverts are adapting to the ectopsychic world in the first half of life, they each do so *very* differently.

Another related problem for the introvert is that in the second half of life, his encounter with his inferior function often plays out in the ectopsychic realm, i.e., out there for everyone to see. Extraverts, on the other hand, have their auxiliary and inferior function playing out more in the endopsychic realm, out of sight. In the second half of life, the extraverts then may seem to "individuate" more discreetly (or repress more) than introverts may. In this way, too, it seems introverts get the "double whammy."

We should quickly comment that both extraverts and introverts ultimately have to deal with the endopsychic as well, and midlife does seem to be the great leveler in this regard, with neither extraverts nor introverts having a privileged status.

The endopsychic field is by definition what is outside consciousness, and having much to do with emotional states and excesses. Introverts, just because they prefer the inner life, are not spared in the individuation process. On this issue a participant in a workshop I was giving on the inferior function and the individuation process recalled a comment that von Franz had made when asked, "How do introverts individuate?" She reportedly said, "With more introversion."

That sounds right. Even though introverts in the second half of life may find much of the unconscious material in the outer world, individuation will still require more introversion, more reflection and work on the inside, as it will for extraverts now also. This "going in" is what for Jung the second half of life is about (though of course it is hoped that one does not get lost inside and never come back out!).

Finally, before moving away from this conceptualization, we would do well to note that the ecto*psychic* and endo*psychic* fields referred to in this Tavistock lecture are both part of "psyche." Jung seems to be implying that both fields are part of and contained by "psyche" as a whole, i.e., the archetypal Self as world and "soul."

Further Differentiating

To conclude this section on type development and the individuation process, I will suggest now a way to distinguish three subcategories of type development in the first half of life. These divisions could serve as a way to come to terms with the different ego-patterns possible from a typological perspective. I use these subcategories to mark off a more or less successful emergence of the ego from the archetypal matrix or collective unconscious, in its most undifferentiated form. These three subcategories then would probably apply most clearly to individuals between the ages of twenty and thirty-five, the fourth stage in the schema above.

When the ego-pattern has developed typologically to include one function (a rational, i.e., either the thinking or feeling function, or an irrational, i.e., either the sensing or intuiting function) in one attitude (either extraversion or introversion), I use the designation, "Simple Type." Using our typological shorthand (I = introversion, N = intuition), examples are as follows:

"Simple Types"

IF	EF
IT	ET
IS	ES
IN	ET

**One function (rational or irrational)
differentiated in one attitude**

As we have stated, to differentiate out an attitude and function type for consciousness is a great achievement. Introverts, however, who rest content with simply differentiating their superior function, will probably not feel comfortable in the ectopsychic field. They are almost always forced to develop a function in the extraverted mode. In the first half of life, extraverts may develop their auxiliary function perhaps a little less "compulsively," or with less anger or resentment, if they do so at all.

When the ego-pattern does include auxiliary functions that promote a balance of extraversion and introversion, with rational and irrational functions respectively, I use the designation "Complex Type." Examples are as follows:

"Complex Types"

EF/IN	ES/IT
EF/IS	ES/IF
ET/IN	EN/IT
ET/IS	EN/IF
IF/EN	IS/ET
IF/ES	IS/EF
IT/EN	IN/ET
IT/ES	IN/EF

**Balance of
Extraversion / Introversion and
Rational / Irrational Functions**

Interestingly, in *Analytical Psychology, the Seminar Given in 1925,* Jung states that most problems in the first half of life have to do with the tension between opposites existing between the two functions vying to be "auxiliary," i.e., vying to "help" the ego to differentiate out of the unconscious and face the world (1989, pp. 82–90). For example, if an individual has differentiated introverted feeling as a superior function, most problems in the first half of life will have to do with the opposition between sensing and intuiting, either in the extraverted or introverted modes, trying to align with the superior introverted feeling function. Through the opposition another function is being differentiated out for consciousness.

Typically for Jung only in the second half of life does one truly get into the problem of opposites involving the superior and inferior function in the classic sense described, for example, in Chapter IV.

When complex ego-patterns have developed outside the two above patterns, I use the designation "Aberrant" or "Unstable Types." In these types, a balance or symmetry between introversion and extraversion, and rational and irrational functions is NOT assumed, as in the case of "Complex Types." I do not mean to suggest anything pathological here, though I believe these ego-patterns break conventions that "Simple Types" and "Complex Types" value implicitly. Examples of "Aberrant" or "Unstable" types are as follows:

"Aberrant" / "Unstable" Types

IF/IT	IT/IF	IS/IN	IN/IS
IF/ET	IT/EF	IS/EN	IN/ES
IF/IN	IT/IN	IS/IT	IN/IT
IF/IS	IT/IS	IS/IF	IN/IF
IF/EF	IT/ET	IS/ES	IN/EN
EF/ET	ET/EF	ES/EN	EN/ES
EF/IT	ET/IF	ES/IN	EN/IS
EF/EN	ET/EN	ES/ET	EN/ET
EF/ES	ET/ES	ES/EF	EN/EF
EF/IF	ET/IT	ES/IS	EN/IN

I hasten to say that names for the three subcategories of ego-patterns as understood through type development are used only as a way to separate out important information in regard to varying ego-structures and type development. These terms or subcategories are not meant to imply any value judgment of one subcategory or ego-pattern as being better than another in any way, shape, or form.

In individual cases I would be inclined to consider any of the three subcategories of ego-patterns in relationship to the whole of the personality, i.e., the archetypal Self, and I would consider the ego-pattern itself, whatever it is, to be of relative (not absolute) importance in regard to what is going on with the individual at a particular time and place in his or her own life.

In the case of the first two subcategories, the terminology reflects my belief that the ego in a majority of cases wants to stabilize itself and can do so most effectively when it has developed one attitude and one function-type (the "Simple Types") or one attitude and a rational function and the other attitude and an irrational function (the "Complex Types"). However, I do not want to take that assumption *too* much for granted.

"Aberrant" or "Unstable" Types are so called from a per-

spective of the ego's need to balance itself out in everyday life
without significant interference from a) intrusive, unconscious elements (being taken over by the endopsychic realm),
or b) whatever the ego feels threatened by in the world. In
other words, I respect the ego's need to maintain its balance
and autonomy, especially in the first half of life, but do not
want to make balance and autonomy an absolute for all individuals in all circumstances.

From this perspective, the "Aberrant" or "Unstable"
types may not be as easy to observe as the "Simple Types,"
nor do they appear to have the symmetry and balance of the
"Complex Types." Once again, only insofar as symmetry and
balance may be desirable qualities in a psychology of consciousness are such types as listed above "Aberrant" or
"Unstable."

A few other comments are in order about this third sub-
category of ego-pattern. "Aberrant" or "Unstable" Types may
also have a greater tolerance of ambiguity, less a need to control inner or outer life, and perhaps a more open/creative attitude toward endopsychic phenomena than types of the other
two categories. The tradeoff here is that these types could
likewise experience life with more volatile emotional shifts
and court a host of psychological issues and problems that
"Simple" or "Complex" Types would seek to avoid as long as
possible.

In terms of working with subcategories one and two, the
MBTI seems appropriate. In terms of working with subcategory three, the SLIP seems useful (see Appendices A and B).

Whatever ego-pattern emerges in an individual as a result
of type development, all other typological dimensions remain
more or less in the unconscious, and can therefore present significant problems to consciousness. For all three subcategories
the inferior function as the absolute opposite of the superior
function in every way represents the most difficult aspect of
type development because it firmly aligns with the unconscious throughout the individuation process. As we have seen,
it will not be made conscious in the sense that the other functions may. All inferior functions therefore serve as doorways
to the archetypal world. Furthermore, while the other dimensions in typological theory can be brought into consciousness
without dramatically changing consciousness itself, working

with any inferior function is always transformational, or as a client of mine said recently, "This work is deadly."

Much has been said on type development and the individuation process. To conclude these thoughts, I am heartened by a closing comment from the 1917 revision of the essay quoted above from Jung's *Collected Papers*. I use this quote in the context of wondering with my clients, as we all proceed through life, why life itself often seems to be so difficult, or even if it is worthwhile at all. As Jung was struggling himself with such issues during his confrontation with the unconscious, he concluded in this essay with the following comment:

> Every pioneer must take his own path, alone but hopeful, with the open eyes of one who is conscious of its solitude and the perils of its dim precipices. Our age is seeking a new spring of life. I found one and drank of it and the water tasted good. That is all that I can or want to say. (*Collected Papers*, 1917, p. 444)

VII

Conclusion:
The Bow and the Lyre

Every individual is an exception to the rule. Hence one can never give a description of a type, no matter how complete, that would apply to more than one individual, despite the fact that in some ways it aptly characterizes thousands of others. Conformity is one side of man, uniqueness is the other.

(CW 6, para. 895)

BECAUSE THE UNCONSCIOUS is constantly a factor and condition of the individual's psychological type, it is much more difficult to determine an individual's type than one might believe or than typological tests may indicate. Functions blur together and attitudes conflate in proportion to how differentiated the personality is and how well the individual's ego has been able to separate from the unconscious. We should not, therefore, move too hastily to impose a false or superficial order on the individual's personality before the individual has had the opportunity to see for him- or herself what is going on, psychologically speaking. Fundamentally, this means we should not short-circuit the workings of the individual's Self in the therapeutic process; we should instead facilitate the natural order appropriate for the individual according to his or her own inner laws. On the difficulty of diagnosing a person's psychological type, Jung himself explains:

The observer sees both the manifestations of the conscious attitude and the autonomous phenomena of the unconscious, and he will be at a loss as to what he should ascribe to consciousness and what to the unconscious. A differential diagnosis can be based only on a careful study of the qualities of the observed material. We must try to discover which phenomena result from consciously chosen motives and which are spontaneous, and it must also be established which of them are adapted, and which of them have an unadapted character. (CW 6, para. 909)

In this regard, before we end this study on Jungian typology we have an earlier promise to keep. In Chapter I, we alluded to a possible corrective to a "creative misreading" of Jung's typology. That misreading was analyzed in terms of an over-identification with the ordering qualities present in Jung's work. We saw that much of what we termed "typological frenzy" could be understood as individuals or groups unconsciously acting out what was referred to as the archetype of order. We briefly examined some aspects of this archetype of order by looking at several attributes of the Greek god Apollo. Finally, we ended the section with a warning about this demanding and powerful figure and how he can distort our uses of Jungian typology. By now, the fact that frenzy should result from too great an emphasis on order should no longer surprise us.

I will conclude our study by reflecting on another mythological figure competitive and akin to Apollo. I am speaking of Apollo's younger brother, Hermes, and am referring through him to the archetype of invention. By "invention," I mean both the act of "inventiveness" as well as the product of an "invention," and similarly "craftiness" along with "craft." The symbol to explore in regard to these attributes of Hermes is the lyre, the musical instrument of his own design, which may be contrasted to Apollo's well-known and characteristic symbol of the bow. Relating Hermes to Apollo at a symbolic level will add the necessary corrective to a reading of *Psychological Types* that could otherwise be dominated by Apollo—i.e., the archetype of order. It follows that we first need to get a sense of who Hermes is and what type of relationship he has with his brother.

Norman O. Brown tells us that Hermes figures in a variety of roles in Greek mythology. Among his epithets are Hermes the Thief, the Shepherd, the Craftsman, the Herald, the Musician, the Athlete, and the Merchant (1969, p. 3). In Homer's *Odyssey*, Hermes is "Guide of Souls." Walter Otto describes this complex god and friend to humans as "the master of ingenuity, the guide of flocks, the friend and lover of the Nymphs and Graces, the spirit of night, sleep, and dreams" (1954, p. 124). In passing, we note also that the Oxford Classical Dictionary states "four is Hermes' number" (recall above the significance of the number four in typological theory, pp. 48–49).

I bring up all these associations and images now to suggest that certain aspects of Jung's typology are better understood through a consideration of these more subtle attributes of Hermes over the grand appeal of Apollo. A particular story comes to mind which can be retold for purposes of amplification on this main theme.

The "Homeric Hymn to Hermes" (Athanassakis, 1976) gives a composite picture of Hermes as a precocious and inventive "baby-god" amazingly adept at scheming to achieve his own ends. Hermes seems especially able at getting his way when situations seem most obviously to play against him.

According to the Hymn, by nightfall on the day of Hermes' birth, this clever god has already hatched a bold scheme to steal fifty head of cattle from his powerful older brother, Apollo. The Hymn seems to imply that the theft was an ambitious move to rival and challenge his more august brother's status and wealth. If successful, the theft would help Hermes to attain his rightful place among the gods. But the deed of course is not without risk.

In the theft, Hermes' plan involves leading the cattle at night through a circuitous route to a remote barn for safe keeping. Along the way, Hermes painstakingly covers the tracks of the herd to avoid possible detection. Then, once the cattle are hidden and safe, Hermes returns to his crib, giving the impression that he had been sleeping at home with his mother during the time of the theft.

Despite Hermes' confidence and clever precautions, Apollo is able to quickly track down the tiny rogue as the mastermind of the crime. However, when questioned and threatened by Apollo about the location of the stolen cattle, Hermes vehemently denies any personal knowledge of the situation and makes fun of Apollo for overestimating a baby's strength and cunning. Hermes even goes so far as to offer to take an oath to allay Apollo's suspicions. But, Apollo, who knows that taking an oath would be to this liar's advantage, decides instead to take Hermes directly to Zeus for swift and just action.

In front of Zeus, Hermes is just as intransigent. However, after being initially amused by Hermes, Zeus finally loses his patience and orders him to guide Apollo to the place where the stolen cows are hidden and to come to some type of accord with his powerful brother for the theft. On Zeus's command, Hermes takes Apollo to the cattle and makes ready to strike a deal.

For our purposes, the Hymn now becomes especially interesting. When the two gods reach the place where the cattle are hidden, Hermes treats Apollo to an impromptu performance on a new invention of his called the lyre, an instrument made from the shell of a tortoise, stalks of reed, oxhide, and seven strings of sheep-gut. Apollo is swept off his feet by the music and becomes immediately covetous of the instrument as well as Hermes' effortless ability to play it (". . . the divine music went through his heart and sweet longing seized him as he listened attentively," lines 421–423).

Because the lyre has such an allure for Apollo, the stolen herd is now a secondary issue. Apollo is won over by Hermes' virtuoso playing and tells him, ". . . your performance is worth fifty cows; I think we will settle our accounts at peace." Perceiving the new situation, Hermes extends to Apollo the gift of the lyre and teaches him how to play it. With Hermes' gift of the lyre, Apollo vows a friendship with Hermes such that "no one else among the immortals to him would be dearer, neither god, nor man descended from Zeus" (lines 525–527).

In the noteworthy reversal in the Hymn, Apollo gives Hermes Apollo's own shepherd staff along with the herd in friendly exchange for the lyre. The staff fittingly becomes one of the representative symbols for Hermes in Greek art, and a reminder to us of this god's clever and subtle nature.[1]

Let us now recall that Heraclitus has a fragment mentioned earlier in our study (see p. 35) which states, "They don't understand how that which differs with itself is in agreement: harmony consists of opposing tension, like that of the bow and lyre." We may recall too that the bow is identified with Apollo (see p. 19).

In the context of the Heraclitian fragment, it would seem that Hermes' "gift" has a function similar to that of the bow, i.e., it acts to demonstrate the paradox of harmony and opposition considered as one phenomenon. For both the bow and the lyre, if the tension in the strings is too slack or too taut, the instrument cannot function, cannot "play." No music is possible; no shot fired accurate.

But of the bow and the lyre, as the Hymn to Hermes makes clear, the lyre has the more subtle and impressive properties. The attributes of the lyre, while connected with the bow, have the overall effect of putting Apollo into a different and oddly more vulnerable frame of mind than that in which we customarily see him. In fact, the great Apollo seems somewhat subdued by Hermes' invention and inventiveness, and becomes less compulsive or intent on retribution. His priorities seem curiously altered and his perspective or point of view is made pliable and receptive through Hermes' introduction and skillful playing of the lyre.

Likewise, when we allow Hermes his place in our typological applications (for us, literally a *herme*neutics), we can better view Jung's conceptual apparatus and definitions as the heuristic tools they were meant to be. Typology can then act to open us up to what we otherwise may not have imagined was there, taking us out of our customary way of viewing things. With Hermes in the typological picture, the priority of order gives way to the instrumental value of typology as a "tool" for broadening understanding, exploration, and enjoyment.

Without realizing the instrumental value of typology as "tool," our typological applications often seem haughty, stiff, or heavy-handed, a consequence of Apollo's too exclusive influence on our readings. But allowing the value of the lyre to act as the balancing metaphor to Apollo's bow (in effect, realizing how much Apollo needs Hermes' instrument), our applications are made light and enjoyable, "interpretive," as a skilled musician may use his instrument to interpret a piece of music and so delight an audience.

At first breath, the ordering effects which typology evokes in the user no doubt conjure the grand attributes of Apollo. People who use typology often experience the same excitement as an archer would have hitting the bull's eye. Jung, in many passages of the *Collected Works*, even substantiates this point of view, as he himself seemed intent on wanting to hit the "target."

However, we would do well now to take a hint from Heraclitus and bring Apollo's bow into creative juxtaposition to Hermes' lyre, to the attributes of Hermes' instrument given to his brother, and to Hermes himself as he is depicted in the hymn to his honor. As metaphors, both the lyre and the bow are vital to understanding Jung's typology: the bow acts as a metaphor for taking one to the mark, hitting the target, experiencing goals, and feeling comfortable in the setting of light, clarity, and order; the lyre acts a metaphor for inventiveness and invention, instrument and tool, spontaneity and subjectivity, boldness and subtlety.

Because the lyre plays such a central role for Apollo, we would do well to realize that the ordering qualities of typology which may be immediately appealing are in fact also vulnerable and subordinate to Hermes' scheming. That is, this subjective and "virtuoso" aspect of typology as a played "instrument" should never be discounted or forgotten in favor of the weapon, the bow.

One who uses typology is always interpreting. Another way of saying this would be to insist that typology is never any better an instrument or tool than the skill of its user, regardless of the ordering effects that may be produced in any of its applications. Jung would say, ". . . the point is not the technique, but the person who uses the technique" (CW 10, para. 337).

The subtle friendship formed between Apollo and Hermes and clarified by the Homeric hymn is analogous to the links between typology and Jungian depth psychology, as the two "brothers" which they are meant to be. Bringing Hermes into the typological picture this way will deepen our respect for the individual, allowing the mystery of the personality the final word.

Fittingly, we will let Hermes' advice to Apollo on the use of his invention and gift guide us toward future applications of Jungian typology:

> Whoever with skill and wisdom expertly asks,
> to him it will speak and teach all manner of
> things joyful to the mind, being played with a gentle
> touch, for it shuns toilsome practice. But, if
> anyone should in ignorance question it at first
> with rudeness, to him in vain it will chatter
> high-flown gibberish forever.
>
> "The Homeric Hymn to Hermes"
> (Athanassakis, 1976, p. 44)

Note

1. Jacobi refers to the staff of Hermes as "an excellent symbol for the transcendent function" (1959, p. 99f), a point that works well with the use we have made of the Hymn to Hermes.

Appendix A

Jungian Typology and the MBTI

THE MYERS-BRIGGS TYPE INDICATOR (MBTI) incorporates a theoretical innovation that brings to Jung's original typological theory something worthy of our attention. This innovation, when brought to bear on Jung's original theory, can be seen as a way to simplify the problems associated with identifying and ranking the four functions within any given psychological type. The Indicator itself is ostensibly designed to identify and measure attitude and function preferences, and by so doing to provide the therapist with some objective confirmation or counterpoint to his or her own typological observations. But the theoretical innovation underlying the Indicator can be considered even apart from the actual use of the MBTI test, and represents a contribution of its own kind to Jungian typological theory.

The MBTI Innovation

If Jung saw the overriding importance of the introversion-extraversion polarity in his typological theory, Briggs-Myers saw the extended significance of the perceiving-judging polarity. It will be remembered that Jung posits four functions that are divided into pairs: the perceiving or irrational functions (sensation and intuition), and the judging or rational functions (thinking and feeling). The innovation brought to bear on typological theory via the MBTI has to do above all with Briggs-Myers' emphasis on and revaluation of this perceiving-judging polarity.

Briggs-Myers considers the perceiving-judging polarity to be intimately and revealingly connected with the introversion-extraversion polarity. Jung specifically states, "The distinction between rational and irrational types (i.e., judging and perceiving types) is simply another point of view and has nothing to do with introversion and extraversion" (CW 6, para. 835). But it is precisely by focusing on the perceiving-judging *polarity* as it relates to introversion and extraversion that Briggs-Myers at once critiques Jung's point of view and extends his theory in another direction.

To quickly review Jung's typological theory: a person's psychological type is composed of one attitude in consciousness (either introversion or extraversion) that is usually characterized by one perceiving function (either sensation or intuition) or one judging function (either thinking or feeling). This superior or dominant function is often helped out by an auxiliary function in the opposite attitude which complements the superior function. If the superior function is one of the judging functions, then the auxiliary function is one of the perceiving functions; if the superior function is one of the perceiving functions, then the auxiliary function is one of the judging functions. In either case, the auxiliary function serves to balance the conscious personality. By including the auxiliary function as part of a person's psychological type, Jung's theory can generate sixteen possible psychological types.

Along with energy moving toward or with consciousness, a countermovement of energy within the personality also takes place at the unconscious level. This movement of energy quickens a kind of counter-personality (an alter-ego or shadow figure) that virtually lives in the unconscious until it is able to force its way out. Because of the neglected and hidden nature of this figure in the unconscious, when it does see the light of day, it characteristically expresses itself with a kind of pent-up energy and primitive power that is troublesome and often antagonistic to the individual and/or others around him. Theoretically, just as there are sixteen possible psychological types, there are sixteen of these troublesome counter-personalities.

However, in practice, unless one is supremely gifted and can "pick up" a person's psychological type in a flash, observing a person to determine his or her psychological type can be, as Jung himself often pointed out, extraordinarily difficult (CW 6, para. 3). The MBTI is an assessment tool which was designed to make an easier and more objective job of identifying and measuring the typological patterns of personality as elaborated by Jung in his typological theory. Faithful users of the Indicator claim that results compiled from the combination of one hundred questions and word-pairs that are presented in forced-choice format to a client will reflect the behaviors of that client that are consistent with a psychological type as described by Jung. The MBTI in effect provides a "read-out" of a person's psychological type.

Common MBTI shorthand for a person's psychological type may be, for example, INFP, i.e., a person whose choices on the Indicator reflect a preference for introversion (I) over extraversion (E), intuition (N) over sensing (S), feeling (F) over thinking (T), and perceiving (P) over judging (J). The Indicator also has psychometric properties that allow for the scoring of the relative strength of each preference through a formula that tabulates the numerical values assigned to each question and word-pair.

Nonetheless, if all of this worked, and often it does, we are still no better off knowing the ranking order of the functions. That is, in the case of the INFP, is the dominant function intuition (N) or feeling (F)? Or, let us suppose someone took the Indicator and came out ESTJ (extraverted, sensing, thinking, judging): would the dominant function be sensing (S) or thinking (T)? Most importantly, what is the purpose of the fourth letter designation P (=perceiving) or J (=judging) in the MBTI read-out? How one answers these questions takes us to the heart of the MBTI innovation.

Briggs-Myers took seriously much of what Jung said about the difficulties which the introvert has in relating to the outside/external world. Briggs-Myers herself was by all accounts an introvert. Along with Jung, she knew very well that because the introvert's energy naturally takes this type of individual to the internal world of ideas and the subjective self, the outside/external world often gets compromised or neglected.

However, Briggs-Myers also did not feel that the information Jung provided on the introversion-extraversion polarity sufficiently explained the typological adaptation that both introverts and extraverts *must* make to the outside world; thus, she went one step further than Jung by typologically characterizing that adaptation. She did this by extending the significance of Jung's perceiving-judging polarity as the main criterion for how one relates to the outside world.

Does the person commonly relate to the world in an open, spontaneous, flowing manner, taking in information at will, avoiding closure or resolution, adapting to circumstance? If so, Briggs-Myers would say that that person's psychological type favors the perceiving (P) end of the perceiving-judging polarity. Or, does the person approach the world seeking system and closure, cutting off information to make a decision, bringing things to order or resolution? If so, Briggs-Myers would say that person's psychological type favors the judging (J) end of the perceiving-judging polarity (Briggs-Myers, 1984, pp. 69–75).

Let us return now to the earlier case of the INFP. The P refers to the perceiving end of the perceiving-judging polarity. This means then that an INFP answered those questions on the Indicator which reflect a preference for meeting the world in a perceiving mode (open, flexible, adaptive, wanting more information, etc.). Since the perceiving function that registered on the Indicator was N (=intuition) and not S (=sensing), the INFP meets the world with intuition.

However, for Briggs-Myers the introversion of the INFP means that the superior or dominant function will be reserved for the internal world. Therefore, intuition in the external world designates the auxiliary (or second-best) function for the INFP. The other function recorded by the Indicator for the INFP is F (=feeling), which acts as the superior function for this particular psychological type.

Further ranking of the functions is structural and consistent with Jung's typological principles. For all types, the tertiary function is opposite to the auxiliary function; therefore, for the INFP the tertiary *sensing* function is opposite to the auxiliary *intuiting* function. For all types, the inferior or fourth function is opposite to the superior function; therefore, for the INFP the inferior *thinking* function is opposite to the superior feeling function.

For demonstration's sake, we will walk through an example for extraverted types. Suppose a type were reported on the Indicator as an ESTJ (extravert, sensing, thinking, judging). The ESTJ faces the external world with the judging end of the judging-perceiving polarity. The judging function for an ESTJ reported on the MBTI is T (=thinking). Because the ESTJ is E (=extravert), the function which the ESTJ uses in the external world will coincide with the ESTJ's superior or dominant function. Therefore, T (=thinking) is the ESTJ's dominant function. The remaining function reported on the Indicator for an ESTJ is S (=sensing), and so serves as the auxiliary or helping function, chiefly operating in the internal world. The opposite of the auxiliary sensing function is the tertiary intuiting function. The opposite of the superior thinking function is the inferior (fourth) feeling function.

The key to using the perceiving-judging polarity is to realize that for an introvert this polarity always refers to an auxiliary function, and for an extravert it always refers to a superior or dominant function. According to Briggs-Myers, introverts keep their favorite or superior function to themselves, in their preferred interior world, and so use their auxiliary function to deal with the outside world. By contrast, extraverts show and use their superior or dominant function in the outside world, which is their preferred world, and thus use their auxiliary function chiefly in the internal world. It will be remembered that the auxiliary function is so designated primarily because of its relatively easy availability to consciousness when a person needs to make use of a complementary function.

By developing the perceiving-judging polarity as a separate criterion and then combining it with Jung's basic typological theory and principles, Briggs-Myers implicitly urges users of Jung's original typological theory to be more careful observers of those patterns of behavior relating specifically to the external world.

Briggs-Myers even seems to suggest a sequence to typological observations: first, determine which particular function seems to be habitually operating in the external world; second, observe whether a person is introverted or extraverted. If the person proves to be introverted, one will have to spend a little more time and effort to find out which function acts as the superior or dominant function operating in the internal world. For the introvert, the more easily observed function represents the auxiliary function. If a person is extraverted, the more easily observed function is the superior or dominant function. In the case of the extravert, one would spend more time finding out which particular function serves as the auxiliary function operating chiefly in the internal world.

Once we have this basic information, we have everything we need to rank all the functions. By applying information from the perceiving-judging polarity with other typological principles and observations (as we did in our two examples above), Briggs-Myers thus provides a theoretical procedure for identifying and ranking the four functions for any type. All this can be done without actually administering the MBTI test.

Some users of Jungian typology will think that the MBTI emphasis on the perceiving-judging polarity as a separate criterion for typological observations confusedly competes with Jung's concept of the *persona*, the archetypal term Jung uses to designate the mask one wears in adapting to the everyday world. This confusion need not be. There are, in fact, sizable differences between the perceiving-judging polarity as Briggs-Myers defines it and Jung's concept of the persona. Jung states, "The persona is a functional complex that comes into existence for reason of adaptation or personal convenience, but is by no means identical with the individuality. The persona is exclusively concerned with the relation to objects" (CW 6, para. 801). Because of this latter mentioned "exclusive concern with objects," one can see where the confusion may occur. However, the more important phrase here refers to the persona as a "functional complex." While the J-P scale in the MBTI can indicate an aspect of the persona, one gets the impression that for Jung persona refers to something more involved. The comparison between these two facets of the everyday personality may be analogous to comparing apples and fruit salad. Also, one suspects that in approaching the persona and the perceiving-judging polarity one could highlight the qualitative differences between "archetype" and "type"; i.e., both terms being related, but each raising different psychological issues.

This all goes to say that the MBTI innovation can be considered separately from Jungian psychology proper, depending first of all upon the necessity to explore the personality in a deeper or more profound manner, as well as the relative capability of the individual's ego to "handle" material from the unconscious. This is a critical distinction to make when comparing both typologies for use with a particular client.

Ultimately, the person using Jungian typology will have to decide first on the legitimacy of the MBTI innovation, then whether it is appropriate and useful in a particular case, and finally whether to employ the MBTI test itself.

The MBTI: Too Tidy a Typology?

For some, Briggs-Myers' reading of *Psychological Types* is both a faithful and creative application of Jung's intentions. Her emphasis on the perceiving-judging polarity is thought to provide the needed "fourth dimension" to round out or complete Jung's psychology of consciousness. For others, the Indicator has had the effect of tightening the spirit of Jung's general psychological work and tying up those "loose ends" through which important material from the unconscious may find its way up. In effect, Jungian typology as incarnated in the MBTI may be trying to say too much about consciousness at the expense of the unconscious.

As we have seen in this study, typology (or any psycho-

logical theory for that matter) in Jung's conception is not
meant to inhibit the experiencing of psychological facts. So,
while there are many advantages to the clarity, structure, and
symmetry of Jung's own theory, he would be the first to say
that if the theory is used to cut off the individual from significant psychological information, then it has outlived its
usefulness. Always of primary importance to Jung is that the
individual using typology be *receptive* to pertinent psychological information as it presents itself from the unconscious.

Concerning Jung's typological theory itself, which James
Hillman has called "the least imagistic of all of (Jung's) major
later works" (1976, p. 245), the further "tidying-up" of typology by proponents of the MBTI may then be reason for some
alarm. The concern here would be, "isn't typology 'too tidy'
already"? And, "wouldn't any further 'tidying up' risk cutting
us off from the image-making potential of the unconscious,
which in turn is vital to the conscious life of the individual"?

As mentioned in Chapter I of our study, Jungian typology
already has a tendency to evoke in many of us the archetype
of order. It should not, for example, strike readers as merely
coincidental that Isabel Briggs-Myers applied her interests in
typology wishing to restore order during World War II (see
p. 12). Nor should one be surprised at the current popularity
of MBTI proponents like Otto Kroeger and Sandra Hirsch,
who have built their own consulting firms around typological workshops geared for organizations such as the War Col-
leges of the Army and Air Force, IBM, AT&T, the IRS, Citi-
corp, Exxon, Ford Motor Company, Honeywell, and a number
of Fortune 500 companies (see Kroeger, 1988, p. xiv, and
Hirsch, 1985, p. 1). In fact, it is safe to predict that typology
via the tidy and palatable rendition given to it by MBTI proponents such as Kroeger and Hirsch (and many others) will
continue to be used to "straighten out" problems and "orga-
nize" organizations for at least another twenty years. Fine.
But, it is these basically well-intentioned applications of
typology that also provide enough evidence to warrant Hillman's otherwise shrill lament about Jungian typology in general. That is, if there is any way that "actual concrete qualities of personality lose their blood to attitudes and
functions," as Hillman puts it (1980, p. 232), then it is
through the too tidy rendition of Jung's original theory cur-

rently in use by many MBTI proponents. In fact, the dramatic and unparalleled success of the MBTI as a veritable training "weapon" must give Hillman himself nightmares.

No doubt some of the three million people taking the MBTI this year will go on to approach Jung's *Psychological Types* with an MBTI bias. As a result, Jung himself will be either more accessible than he should be (i.e., too easy to do anyone any real psychological good), or too difficult to deal with (and therefore easy to ignore). While the latter often happens (see Kroeger, 1988, p. 8), it should be noted that such a viewpoint is not the official position of most MBTI proponents. That is, most individuals using the MBTI graciously acknowledge Jung and often refer to his original theory for a kind of sustenance and challenge.

Yet this is also precisely and ironically the point. Because of the essentially pro-Jung stance of many MBTI proponents (again, well-intentioned), one grows especially nervous about all the "business" of typology being conducted in Jung's name. One indeed cannot easily separate the resurgence of interest in Jung's theory (now over seventy years old) from the incredible growth of activity that continues to take place around the MBTI itself. Undeniably, the MBTI, more so than other Jungian-based typological "tests," such as the Grey-Wheelwright and the Singer-Loomis, is curiously linked to the general popularity of Jung's typological theory. By a kind of metonymic reduction, some MBTI proponents assume a kind of "prime mover" status for the increase in interest and publications concerning Jungian typology specifically, if not Jungian psychology generally. One can only recall here the folk tale of the fisherman calmly fishing for minnows from atop the back of a whale. The fact that the fisherman in this case is busy catching fish does not excuse his lack of knowledge or naivete about the big fish underneath that is supporting him.

My own position on the issue of "too tidy a typology" rests somewhere in between an Otto Kroeger's confidence and a James Hillman's concern. Kroeger gives the most thoroughly "extraverted," "upbeat," and naive version of typology that has come out of the MBTI camp to date. The "whale," Jungian psychology itself or the unconscious, is something that Kroeger feels will not bother him if he does not bother it, and so he understands and uses typology accordingly.

Hillman, in trying to revalue typology in the name of archetypal psychology, is at times downright apocalyptic about typology, which becomes for him a caricature of Jungian psychology, more likely to draw one away from rather than toward the significant psychological (read unconscious) issues.

The differences between the two men are those between day and night. Indeed, typologically speaking, there is every good possibility that Hillman and Kroeger are sizable "shadow" figures for each other. If that is the case, anyone interested in the future of Jungian typology would benefit from looking at both of these figures, and finding a middle way between them.

Appendix B

Jungian Typology and the SLIP

THE SINGER-LOOMIS Inventory of Personality (SLIP) refers to
Jung's original eight psychological types as "cognitive
modes" (e.g., introverted thinking is one cognitive mode,
extraverted sensing another, etc.). As a test, the SLIP is much
more fluid in design than the MBTI, allowing for varying
combinations of cognitive modes to be reported, which when
scored and ranked indicate a unique interactive pattern
referred to as the person's "cognitive style." This innovation,
when brought to bear on Jung's original typological theory, is
a way to preserve maximum ambiguity of one's psychological
type without losing typological definition and description.

In a letter in the original Swiss edition of his autobiography, *Memories, Dreams, Reflections*, Jung comments:

> I strive quite consciously and deliberately for ambiguity of
> expression, because it is superior to singleness of meaning
> and reflects the nature of life . . . I purposely allow all the

overtones and undertones to chime in, because they are there anyway while at the time giving a fuller picture of reality. (quoted in Jaffé, 1984, p. 160f)

The SLIP, created by two Jungian analysts, could be seen as coming out of Jung's own insistence that typology not be used in too heavy-handed or restrictive a fashion and that necessary ambiguity be honestly admitted and honestly preserved. For making this point the SLIP deserves our special attention.

The SLIP Innovation

The creators of the SLIP believe that every individual personality is capable of using and developing at random any of the four typological functions in either of the two attitudes. A typological testing instrument should therefore be able to reflect not only a person's chief typological preferences (e.g., superior introverted feeling with auxiliary extraverted sensing), but also all the remaining functions and attitudes and how they are interacting in the personality. The way the Singer-Loomis goes about meeting this goal is by separately measuring each cognitive mode (e.g., extraverted thinking, introverted sensing, extraverted feeling, etc.)

Measuring for cognitive modes on an independent basis effectively challenges the bipolar assumption of other typological instruments, such as the MBTI and the pioneer of typological tests, the Gray-Wheelwright *Jungian Type Survey*. For purposes of understanding the SLIP, polar opposition between the attitude types (introversion-extraversion), the rational functions (thinking-feeling), and the irrational functions (sensing-intuiting) should only be viewed as the theoretical background which led Jung to his typological formulations and definitions in the first place. In the SLIP, the exclusivity of choice between polar opposites is downplayed in favor of the inclusive (creative, practical) tendencies of the personality to independently utilize and develop all elements of his or her typological makeup.

Singer and Loomis believe that Jung's typological model, at least as we have interpreted it in this study, has a balance and symmetry that is not *necessarily* or *consistently* applicable to everyone in real life. That is, a person's conscious psychological type is not necessarily composed of a perceiving function in one attitude balanced by a judging function in the opposite attitude. Nor would the person's unconscious counter-personality be structurally defined on the basis of the bipolar assumption. Instead, a person may easily and naturally favor any arrangement of cognitive modes independent of one another. In turn, the counter-personality would be composed of the least favored cognitive modes.

For example, extraverted thinking, extraverted feeling, extraverted sensing, and introverted thinking may be favored as the top four cognitive modes, with the remaining four cognitive modes falling somewhere below and ranked in descending order, though still a part of the personality's cognitive style. Polar opposition is therefore not a structural principle determining one's typological profile. To the "either-or" aspect present in typological theory, the Singer-Loomis points to the possibilities of "both-and" in typological practice.

To measure the cognitive modes independently of one another, the SLIP eliminates the forced-choice format that reflects the bipolar assumption in typological tests such as the MBTI and the Gray-Wheelwright. The SLIP instead is designed around fifteen separate "situations" which utilize a series of eight typologically based questions or "indicators" to be answered according to a sliding frequency scale of 1–5, "never to always." "Free response" of this kind has produced for many individuals typological results which openly contradict the outcomes of typological tests using a forced-choice format. It is not unusual to even find the superior function reported from one test format to be different from the superior function reported in the other (Singer and Loomis, 1987, pp. 434–438, 1984a, pp. 9–10).

Singer and Loomis would suggest that the SLIP, by allowing for a free and creative "mix" of various cognitive modes, both more accurately conveys the range and intentions of Jung's typological theory and better reflects typological facts in the everyday world. Should a particular structural dynam-

ic based on the bipolar assumption be a part of the typological makeup of the person, the SLIP can reflect that fact. But
more importantly, if this particular structure is *not* present in
the individual's typological makeup, the SLIP can reflect that
fact as well.

In other words, it may turn out that a person's superior
cognitive mode is introverted thinking, the auxiliary cognitive mode extraverted sensing, the tertiary cognitive mode
extraverted intuiting, and the inferior cognitive mode
extraverted feeling. These four modes would be the equivalent of what we would term, in a structural fashion, "an
introverted thinking-type with sensing whose counter-personality is extraverted feeling with intuition." This psychological type, reflecting in practice the balance and symmetry
that is suggested in Jung's typological theory, indeed exists
and as such could be registered on the SLIP.

But, Singer and Loomis would suggest, it is also possible
that a person could have as easily turned out a different combination of cognitive modes, reflecting a different or "non-
structured" typology. For example, the superior cognitive
mode could have been introverted thinking, the auxiliary
cognitive mode introverted feeling, the tertiary cognitive
mode extraverted sensing, and the inferior cognitive mode
extraverted thinking. Such a type may be thought of as structurally out of synch with the assumptions of this study. Or
perhaps more to the point, such a type would seem to have
its own unique structure. The SLIP could not only record
such a unique pattern, it would also point out that the four
cognitive modes reported above are still only half of the eight
that are used by and available to the personality. According to
the SLIP, the psychological types described above would each
have four other independent cognitive modes that only the
SLIP itself could properly account for.

Naturally, with the evaluation of cognitive modes on an
independent basis, the number of possible typological profiles (cognitive styles) far exceeds the sixteen implicit in
Jung's original work and explicit in the work of Myers-Briggs.
The *Interpretive Guide for The Singer-Loomis Inventory of
Personality* (Experimental Edition, 1984) provides twenty-
eight typological profiles composed of combinations based on
the top *two* cognitive modes, the "leading cognitive mode"

(i.e., the superior function) and the "second-cognitive mode" (i.e., the auxiliary function). There is also in the guide an insightful section describing the "least-developed cognitive mode" (i.e., the inferior function).

The SLIP: Too loose a Typology?

The premise of the SLIP is an exciting one, if a bit messy. Oddly enough, however, the SLIP seems to work best when one keeps the bipolar assumption active in the theoretical background of Jung's typology. Doing so allows for the recognition of the *coincedentia oppositorium* that takes place in the personality and is at the heart of Jung's work. This is ultimately the SLIP's great achievement and could be explained as follows.

We have seen that with the SLIP, a person may reflect high preferences for functions that otherwise would not enjoy typological proximity to one another. For example, in our study superior extraverted thinking is structurally linked to inferior introverted feeling as a polar opposite. However, the SLIP indicates that superior extraverted thinking could have introverted feeling as its second cognitive mode. That is, introverted feeling would not be automatically consigned to being reported as an "inferior function"; in fact, in this example it is regarded as the "auxiliary function." Theoretically, any of the remaining six "cognitive modes" could prove to be the "inferior function" or the "least-developed cognitive mode."

Keeping our example and the bipolar assumptions in mind, we realize that the SLIP is able to identify dynamic typological oppositions. Presuming that the superior function is accurately reported, having opposite functions as the top two cognitive modes is tantamount to bringing a person's creative use of such typological opposition into focus. This feature of the instrument reflects the authors' intention to have a typological instrument in which "the interactions of cognitive modes can be examined in terms of their potential for creativity" (1984b, p. 21). Not surprisingly, typology understood in this vein can easily take the therapist and the client into issues relating to the "transcendent function" and the creative life. The SLIP then is capable of providing a significantly different perspective on the personality as a whole.

Because the concern of Singer and Loomis is specifically with the individuation process and not simply typology *per se,* they are able to draw our attention in that direction. The SLIP is thus an ideal tool for connecting typology to Jung's larger psychological model. Singer and Loomis comment:

> Individuation is the process of expanding the personality to include both opposites of a pair. The transcendent function can be born when one is willing to stand in the center of one's circle typologically and bear the tension of developing an inferior function. (1987, p. 440)

Singer and Loomis seem to feel that there are many people who are being misrepresented by typology interpreted through the bipolar assumption. These are individuals who are being forced into a typological structure and dynamic not in keeping with their creative abilities and gifts. For this group, the SLIP seems to be an ideal instrument.

Others, however, will not be able to tolerate what seems to be type theory in deteriorated form, or, what may amount to the same thing, the ambiguity of their own creative lives. In one sense, everyone has the potential to lead the creative life for which the SLIP may help to delineate the typological shape and pattern. The SLIP may even be able to provide a way of "tracking" the individuation process, thereby giving a better sense of that hypothetical "middle ground" in which the transcendent function operates. But, for people who are not at such a point in their individuation process, the methodological design of the SLIP could be disorienting or distracting.

The authors correctly point to the SLIP'S abilities in assessing "the subtle shifting in the blending and fusion of attitude and function" (1987, p. 440). Still, some clients would interpret such subtlety too defensively. The notion of "cognitive style" then becomes too unwieldy to maneuver, viewed as having too many "parts" to account for, causing the person's sense of him- or herself to become fuzzy. In these instances, there would seem to be no hypothetical "steady-point" for ego-consciousness to find its bearings. Such is the price some may pay for the "freedom" the SLIP allows.

At this point perhaps a general comparative statement may be risked in regard to the relative merits of both the MBTI and the SLIP. The SLIP is an instrument that can best be keyed to problems and issues relating specifically to the Archetypal Self and the creative life; the MBTI is very helpful on problems relating to ego-consciousness and the development of the conscious side of one's psychological type. Some clients may benefit more from one test than the other, depending, oddly enough, on the state of their typology. From the point of view of the client, should one instrument earn his or her decided recognition, it should serve as the preferred therapeutic tool, as either instrument is workable in a therapeutic setting and both can help further the individuation process. But both instruments together still do not replace the experience or typological acumen of the competent and attentive therapist who has thoroughly explored his or her own psychological type.

A Typological Glossary

CAVEAT LECTOR: The following definitions pay less attention to the surface of the personality than to the more complex "layers" or "regions" of the psyche which condition and represent the personality in the individuation process. As the function of this glossary is primarily heuristic, I decided that it would be more helpful to arrange our definitions to suggest the widening or deepening of consciousness that ideally would characterize a typological approach to personality. Therefore, in our glossary the less useful criteria of alphabetizing and defining terms has given way to a shape which loosely parallels the shape of our study. Terms that have archetypal significance are italicized.

persona—The "actor's mask" which serves to mediate between an individual's ego and the external reality that delimits an individual's everyday life. Essentially, the *persona* is a functional complex which is represented by the external concession(s) or adaptation(s) that society requires from an individual to make life hospitable or bearable for all concerned. As such, the *persona* may benefit both society and the individual, provided that the individual's life is not reduced (or elevated) to what the *persona* itself comes to represent.

ego (ego complex)—The center, central complex, or carrier of consciousness. The apparent source of will and memory. The "battlefield" between a person's conscious and unconscious life. The ego is especially concerned with problems of personal identity, reality testing, and continuity over time. As such, it simultaneously faces outward toward external reality and inward toward internal reality.

consciousness—The realm of psychic experience for which the ego generally claims a certain degree of relation and level of awareness. As such, consciousness is always "consciousness of," as the phenomenologist Edmund Husserl might have said. In effect, this means largely that the chief characteristic of consciousness is discrimination and differentiation of "this from that."

differentiation—Differentiation "is the essence, the *sine qua non* of consciousness" (CW 7, para. 339). It is psychological activity which separates, untangles, and distinguishes one thing from another.

attitude—Typologically speaking, a fundamental or *a priori* orientation of the personality in which libido either moves toward the object and away from the subject (extraversion) or is withdrawn from the object and put back into the interests of the subject (introversion).

libido—Psychic energy which directs and motivates the personality. The source of libido is the polar nature of the psyche itself, most completely expressed through the myriad interactions and oppositions that exist between an individual's conscious and unconscious life. When an excess of libido is habitually taken up by consciousness in a certain direction or for a certain purpose, the ideal psychic balance or flow between the conscious and unconscious life of the organism is disturbed. A countermovement or buildup of energy then takes place in the unconscious, which seeks to create a new balance for the individual personality. However, the results of this new movement of the psyche to regulate itself often involve primitive or archaic layers of the unconscious itself for which consciousness is ill-prepared to confront. Insofar as this occurs, the route to reorganization and reintegration of one's personality is problematic.

function—A particular form of psychological activity that is recognizable in principle while operating under varying conditions. Typologically speaking, Jung specifies four basic functions: sensation and intuition, which are referred to as irrational or perceiving functions, and thinking and feeling, which are referred to as rational or judging functions. Any function may be introverted or extraverted, depending upon its orientation to the object.

> **sensing function**—One of the two irrational or perceiving functions, so designated because of characteristic openness to information taken in by the senses.

> **intuiting function**—One of the two irrational or perceiving functions, so designated because of characteristic openness to meanings and symbols taken in through the unconscious.

> **thinking function**—One of the two rational or judging functions, so designated because of characteristic activity that uses and applies logic and abstract analysis to a problem.

feeling function—One of the two rational or judging functions, so designated because of characteristic activity that uses and applies subjective values to issues of personal concern.

psychological type—A specific combination of habitually conscious activity that may be identified according to typological principles and concepts. Each individual potentially constellates a particular typological configuration at the conscious level that in turn is compensated at the unconscious level.

superior function—The primary or dominant function which generally represents the most confident and comfortable aspect of the conscious personality. It is the most differentiated function of the personality, and therefore commonly thought to be the most reliable and efficient function from the *ego's* point of view. The carrier of the ego.

auxiliary function—The function which in many cases is sufficiently differentiated to assist or complement the superior function, and so serves to round off or stabilize the *ego* and consciousness. The auxiliary function is a rational (judging) function if the superior function is irrational (perceiving). On the other hand, the auxiliary function may be an irrational (perceiving) function if the superior function is rational (judging).

tertiary function—This term is not used by Jung, but serves to designate the function which is opposite to the auxiliary function. Most often, Jung refers to this function as one of the inferior functions, i.e., a poorly differentiated function associated with the unconscious.

inferior function—The function which is opposite in every way to the superior function, the least reliable, least differentiated, and least characteristic function of the personality. The inferior function most often acts as the doorway through which various aspects of the unconscious may meet, encroach upon, or engulf the ego.

unconscious—A psychological concept which represents all psychic contents or processes that are not related to the ego or consciousness in any immediately perceptible way.

complex—An emotionally charged unconscious psychic entity that is signaled by its apparent autonomy and by the intense affect associated with it in everyday life. Complexes are said to have arche-typal images and patterning at their core.

archetype—The central core of a complex, a transpersonal or uni-versal pattern of experience represented by certain primordial, mythological, or numinous images and often expressed through certain patterns of emotion and behavior.

shadow—The archetype which is represented by everything which the ego has no wish to be. Most commonly, the *shadow* is taken to be the dark side of one's personality and so hidden or excluded from the "light" of consciousness.

transcendent function—The spontaneous and mediating function that links consciousness and the unconscious through the genera-tion and creation of symbols. As such, the transcendent function goes beyond the point of view expressed by any two opposites which may be at the source of psychological conflict.

symbol—An image or metaphor which provides a living perspective from which a synthesis between opposing or conflicting psycholog-ical factors may be considered, reflected, or acted upon. As such, symbols provide meaning and order to our individual and collective lives.

psyche—The whole of one's personality comprising the various contents and relationships that exist between conscious and uncon-scious life.

Self—The center of the psyche, as the ego is the center of con-sciousness. Insofar as it is made conscious by the ego, the *Self* may be viewed (paradoxically) as both the center and circumference of the whole of one's personality. *Ego-Self* relations are therefore always thought of as ongoing and never complete. The *Self* as an archetype is most commonly represented through unifying images that convey the awe and wonder of the "wholly other," or in more obvious language, "the God within." As such, the *Self* also acts meaningfully in directing an individual's life or shaping a person's individual destiny.

Bibliography

Agee, J. (1960). *Let Us Now Praise Famous Men*. Cambridge, Mass.: Riverside Press.

Athanssakis, A. N. (trans.) (1976). *The Homeric Hymns*. Baltimore: Johns Hopkins University Press.

Bennet, E. A. (1962). *C. G. Jung*. New York: E. P. Dutton.

Bolen, J. (1984). *Goddesses in Everywoman*. San Francisco: Harper and Row.

_____ (1989). *Gods in Everyman*. San Francisco: Harper and Row.

Briggs-Myers, I. (1984). *Gifts Differing*. Palo Alto: Consulting Psychologists Press.

Brome, V. (1978). *Jung: Man and Myth*. New York: Atheneum.

Brown, N. (1969). *Hermes the Thief*. New York: Vintage Books.

Campbell, J. (ed.) (1969–1982). *Papers from the Eranos Yearbooks*. Bollingen Series XXX, vols. 1–6. Princeton: Princeton University Press.

Capra, F. (1975). *The Tao of Physics*. Boulder, Colo.: Shambhala Publications.

Edinger, E. F. (1984). *The Creation of Consciousness: Jung's Myth for Modern Man*. Toronto: Inner City Books.

_____ (1972). *Ego and Archetype*. New York: Putnam.

Ellenberger, H. (1970). *The Discovery of the Unconscious*. New York: Basic Books.

Fairbairn, W. (1954). *An Object Relations Theory of the Personality*. New York: Basic Books.

Freeman, K. (1957). *Ancilla to the Pre-socratic Philosophers*. Cambridge, Mass.: Harvard University Press.

Gadamer, H. G. (1976). *Philosophical Hermeneutics*, Berkeley: University of California Press.

Guntrip, H. (1969). *Schizoid Phenomena, Object Relations and the Self*. New York: International Universities Press.

Hannah, B. (1976). *Jung: His Life and Work*. New York: Perigee Books.

Henderson, J. (1982). History and practice of Jungian analysis. In M. Stein (ed.), *Jungian Analysis*. Boulder, Colo.: Shambhala Publications.

Hillman, J. (1983). *Archetypal Psychology*. Dallas: Spring Publications.

———— (1980). Egalitarian typologies versus the perception of the unique. In *Eranos Yearbook 1976*, vol. 45. Netherlands: E. J. Brill.

Hirsch, S. (1985). *Using the Myers-Briggs Type Indicator in Organizations*. Palo Alto: Consulting Psychologists Press.

Homans, P. (1979). *Jung in Context*. Chicago: The University of Chicago Press.

Huizinga, J. (1955). *Homo Ludens: A Study of the Play Element in Culture*. Boston: Beacon Press.

Hull, R. F. C., and McGuire, W. (eds.) (1977). *C.G. Jung Speaking: Interviews and Encounters*. Bollingen Series XCVII. Princeton: Princeton University Press.

Jacobi, J. (1959). *Complex, Archetype, Symbol*. Bollingen Series LVII. New York: Pantheon.

———— (1967). *The Way of Individuation*. New York: Harcourt, Brace & World.

———— (1953). *Psychological Reflections*. Bollingen Series XXXI. New York: Pantheon.

Jaffé, A. (1971). *From the Life and Work of C. G. Jung*. New York: Harper & Row.

———— (1977). Jung at the eranos conferences. In J. Hillman (ed.) *Spring, 1977*, pp. 201–212. Zürich: Spring Publications.

———— (1979). *C. G. Jung: Word and Image*. Bollingen Series XCVII: 2. Princeton: Princeton University Press.

———— (1984). *The Myth of Meaning*. Einsiedeln: Daimon Verlag.

Jung, C. G. (1959, 1975). *Aion*. CW 9ii.

———— (1989). *Analytical Psychology, the Seminar Given in 1925*. Princeton: Princeton University Press.

———— (1970). *Civilization in Transition*. CW 10.

———— (1917). *Collected Papers*. New York: Moffat Yard.

———— (1954). The development of personality. In *CW* 17.

———— (1923, 1977). *Psychological Types*. CW 6.

_____ (1958). *Psychology and Religion: East and West. CW* 11.

_____ (1960, 1969). *The Structure and Dynamics of the Psyche. CW* 8.

_____ (1953, 1966). *Two Essays on Analytical Psychology. CW* 7.

Jung, C. G., and Jaffé, A. (ed.) (1973). *Memories, Dreams, Reflections.* New York: Pantheon.

Kabir (Robert Bly, trans.) (1977). *The Kabir Book.* Boston: Beacon Press.

Keen, S. (1986). *Faces of the Enemy.* San Francisco: Harper and Row.

Kerr, J. (1993). *A Dangerous Method.* New York: Knopf.

Kroeger, O. and Thuesen, J. (1988). *Type Talk, or How to Determine Your Personality Type and Change Your Life.* New York: Delacorte Press.

McCaulley, M. (1980, July). An appreciation of Isabel Briggs Myers. *MBTI News.*

Meier, C. A. (1971). Psychological types and individuation: a plea for a more scientific approach in Jungian psychology. In Wheelwright, J. (ed.), *The Analytic Process: Aims, Analysis, and Training* (pp. 276–289). New York: Putnam.

Otto, W. (1954). *The Homeric Gods.* Boston: Beacon Press.

Pagels, H. (1983). *The Cosmic Code.* New York: Bantam Books.

Perry, J. W. (1953, 1987). *The Self in Psychotic Process.* Dallas: Spring Publications.

Quenk, A. T. (1984). *Psychological Types and Psychotherapy.* Gainesville, Fla.: Center for the Application of Psychological Types.

Rilke, R. M. (Robert Bly, trans.) (1981). *Selected Poems of Rainer Maria Rilke.* New York: Harper & Row.

Rolfe, E. (1989). *Encounter with Jung.* Boston: Sigo Press.

Samuels, A., Shorter, B., and Plaut, A. (1986). *A Critical Dictionary of Jungian Analysis.* London: Routledge and Kegan Paul.

Singer, J. (1982). The education of the analyst. In M. Stein (ed.), *Jungian Analysis.* Boulder, Colo.: Shambhala Publications.

Singer, J. and Loomis, M. (1987). An update on the Singer-Loomis Inventory of Personality. In M. A. Matoon, ed., *The Archetype of Shadow in a Split World: The Tenth International Congress of Analytical Psychology, Berlin.* Einsiedeln, Switzerland: Daimon Verlag, pp. 431–443.

_____ (1984). *The Singer-Loomis Inventory of Personality Manual* (experimental edition). Palo Alto: Consulting Psychologists Press.

_____ (1984). *Interpretive Guide for the Singer-Loomis Inventory of Personality* (experimental edition). Palo Alto: Consulting Psychologists Press.

_____ (1984). The Singer-Loomis inventory of personality: an update of the measurement of Jung's typology (workshop). In M. A. Mattoon (ed.), *The Archetype of the Shadow in a Split World*. Einsiedein: Daimon Verlag.

Stern, P. J. (1976). *C. G. Jung: The Haunted Prophet*. New York: Braziller.

Stevens, A. (1983). *Archetypes: A Natural History of the Self*. New York: Quill Publications.

Talbot, M. (1980). *Mysticism and the New Physics*. New York: Bantam.

_____ (1988). *Beyond the Quantum*. New York: Bantam.

van der Post, I. (1975). *Jung and the Story of Our Time*. New York: Random House.

von Franz, M.-L. (1975). *C. G. Jung: His Myth in Our Time*. New York: Putnam.

_____ (1985). *Projection and Re-collection in Jungian Psychology*. La Salle and London: Open Court.

von Franz, M.-L. and Hillman, J. (1984). *Lectures on Jung's Typology*. Dallas: Spring Publications.

Wehr, G. (1971). *Portrait of Jung*. New York: Herder and Herder.

_____ (1987). *Jung: a Biography*. Boston: Shambhala Publications.

Whitmont, E. (1978). *The Symbolic Quest*. Princeton: Princeton University Press.

Wilhelm, R. (trans.) (1975). *The Secret of the Golden Flower*. New York: Causeway Books.

Winnicott, E. W. (1965). *The Maturational Processes and the Facilitating Environment*. New York: International Publications.

_____ (1971). *Playing and Reality*. London: Tavistock.

Wolff, T. (1956). *Structural Forms of the Feminine Psyche*. Zurich: Students' Association of the C. G. Jung Institute.

Zukav, G. (1979). *The Dancing Wu-Li Masters*. New York: William Morrow.

Index

active imagination, 10, 134–139
    see also transcendent function
adaptation, 28, 43, 130, 176, 178
Adler, Alfred, xix, 4–6
Agee, James, 100
anima/animus, 120, 139, 143
    see also archetype
Apollo, 19, 20, 166–171
APT, *see* Association for
    Psychological Type
APT/CAPT qualifying workshop, 9
ARAS, *see* Archive for Research in
    Archetypal Symbolism
archetype, 18–20, 83, 85, 94, 123,
    124, 126, 129, 137, 144, 150, 166,
    179, 180, 194
    of invention, 166
    of order, 19, 20, 166, 167
Archive for Research in Archetypal
    Symbolism (ARAS), 15
Association for Psychological Type
    (APT), xv, xvi, 8–10, 17, 23
attitude, 5, 28–30, 32–34, 36, 38,
    49–52, 62, 80, 104, 115, 122, 133,
    135, 144, 154, 159, 160–162, 166,
    173, 174, 184, 185, 188, 192
auxiliary function, 49–52, 62–64, 80,
    82, 84, 85, 91, 157, 160, 174, 177,
    178, 187, 193

balance, xii, 37, 38, 80, 121–123,
    146, 160, 162, 174, 185, 186
Bertine, 14
bipolar assumption, 184–188
    see also polarity
Bollingen, xix, 10, 21, 54
Briggs, Katherine, x, xi, xv, xviii,
    7–9, 11, 12, 173, 186
Briggs-Myers, Isabel, 53, 174,
    176–180
Brown, Norman O., 167
Bulletin of Psychological Type, 8

CAPT, *see* Center for Applications
    of Psychological Type
Center for Applications of
    Psychological Type (CAPT),
    8–10, 17
    mission statement, 8
characteristic preferences, 34
child archetype, 137
cognitive mode, 183, 184, 186, 187
cognitive style, 183, 185, 188
collective unconscious, xvi, 10, 80,
    86, 101, 117, 120, 143, 144, 150,
    159
complex, xi, 33, 48, 73, 89, 131,
    143, 144, 155, 160–162, 167, 178,
    179, 193
consciousness, xvii, 3, 5, 6, 20, 23,
    33, 36–43, 49–52, 62, 73, 75–78,
    80–87, 89, 90, 91, 92, 98,
    100–104, 106, 109, 110, 112–135,
    137–139, 142–148, 150, 154–158,
    160, 162, 166, 174, 177, 179, 189,
    191
    Eastern vs. Western
        consciousness, 112–118
conscious-unconscious polarity, 41
    see also polarity
conversation, 60, 63–72, 73
counter-personality, 50, 52, 54, 55,
    63, 83, 85, 89, 175, 185, 186
    see also shadow

dark side, xvii, 78, 87–89, 98, 104,
    129, 131
    see also inferior function
depth psychology, 117, 126, 142,
    170
differentiation, 42, 102, 145, 192
dominant function, 51, 62, 174–178
    see also superior function
dreams, 2, 47, 89, 90, 103, 111, 127,
    132, 141, 167, 183